SIR JOHN MACDONALD
LORD KINGSBURGH

To Neil
with all Best Wishes

Norman

NORMAN MACDONALD

Self-published in 2010
With the aid of:

The Lumphanan Press
5 Auldhill Road
Bridgend
West Lothian
EH49 6PD
thelumphananpress@hotmail.com

ISBN: 978-0-9566149-0-2

Set in Palatino Linotype

Printed and bound in the UK by the MPG Books Group,
Bodmin and King's Lynn

And one man in his time plays many parts

– Shakespeare

For Jill and all the family

CONTENTS

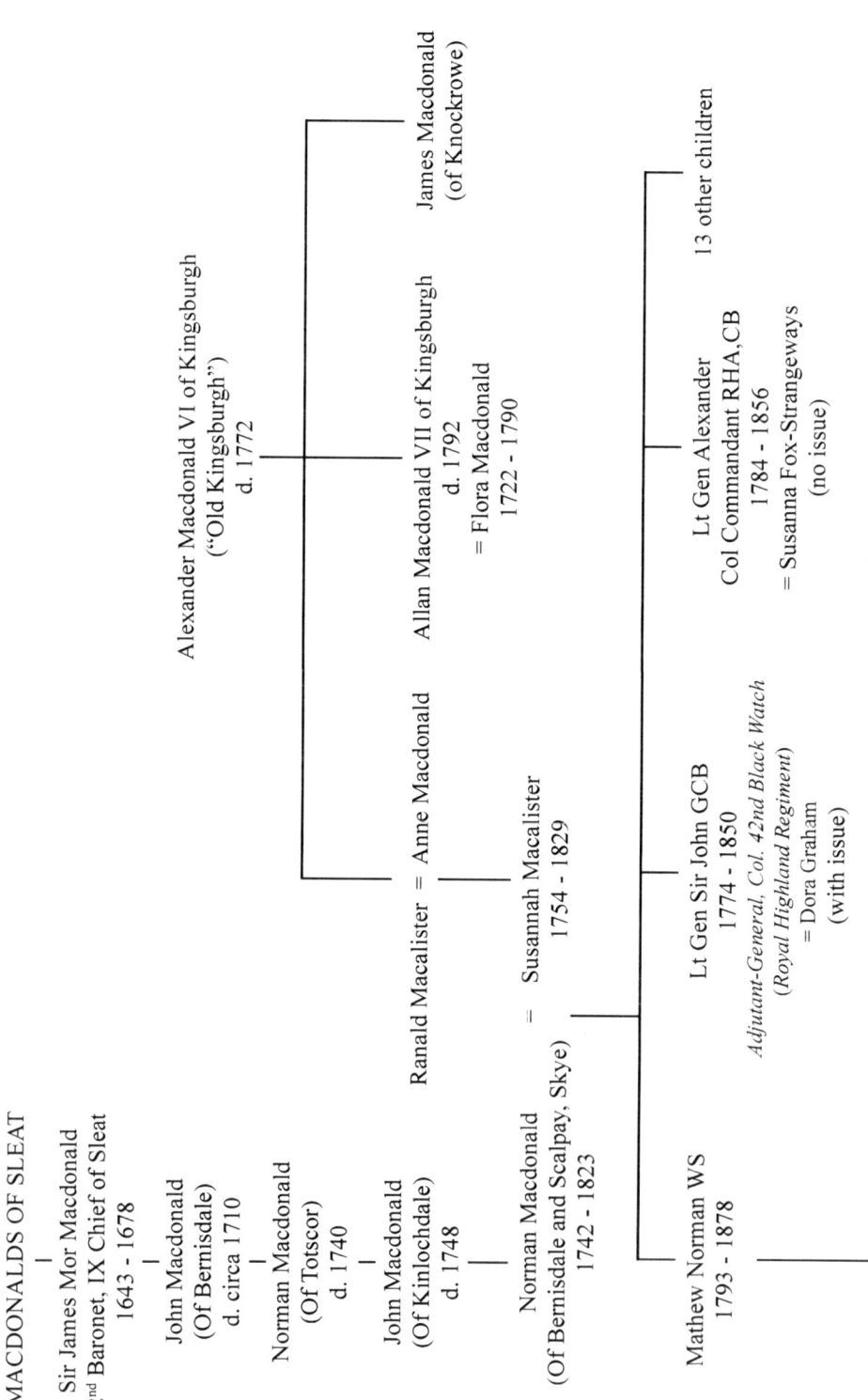

MACDONALDS OF SLEAT

Sir James Mor Macdonald
2nd Baronet, IX Chief of Sleat
1643 - 1678
|
John Macdonald
(Of Bermisdale)
d. circa 1710
|
Norman Macdonald
(Of Totscor)
d. 1740
|
John Macdonald
(Of Kinlochdale)
d. 1748
|
Norman Macdonald
(Of Bermisdale and Scalpay, Skye)
1742 - 1823

Alexander Macdonald VI of Kingsburgh
("Old Kingsburgh")
d. 1772

Allan Macdonald VII of Kingsburgh
d. 1792
= Flora Macdonald
1722 - 1790

James Macdonald
(of Knockrowe)

Ranald Macalister = Anne Macdonald

= Susannah Macalister
1754 - 1829

Lt Gen Sir John GCB
1774 - 1850
Adjutant-General, Col. 42nd Black Watch
(Royal Highland Regiment)
= Dora Graham
(with issue)

Lt Gen Alexander
Col Commandant RHA,CB
1784 - 1856
= Susanna Fox-Strangeways
(no issue)

13 other children

Mathew Norman WS
1793 - 1878

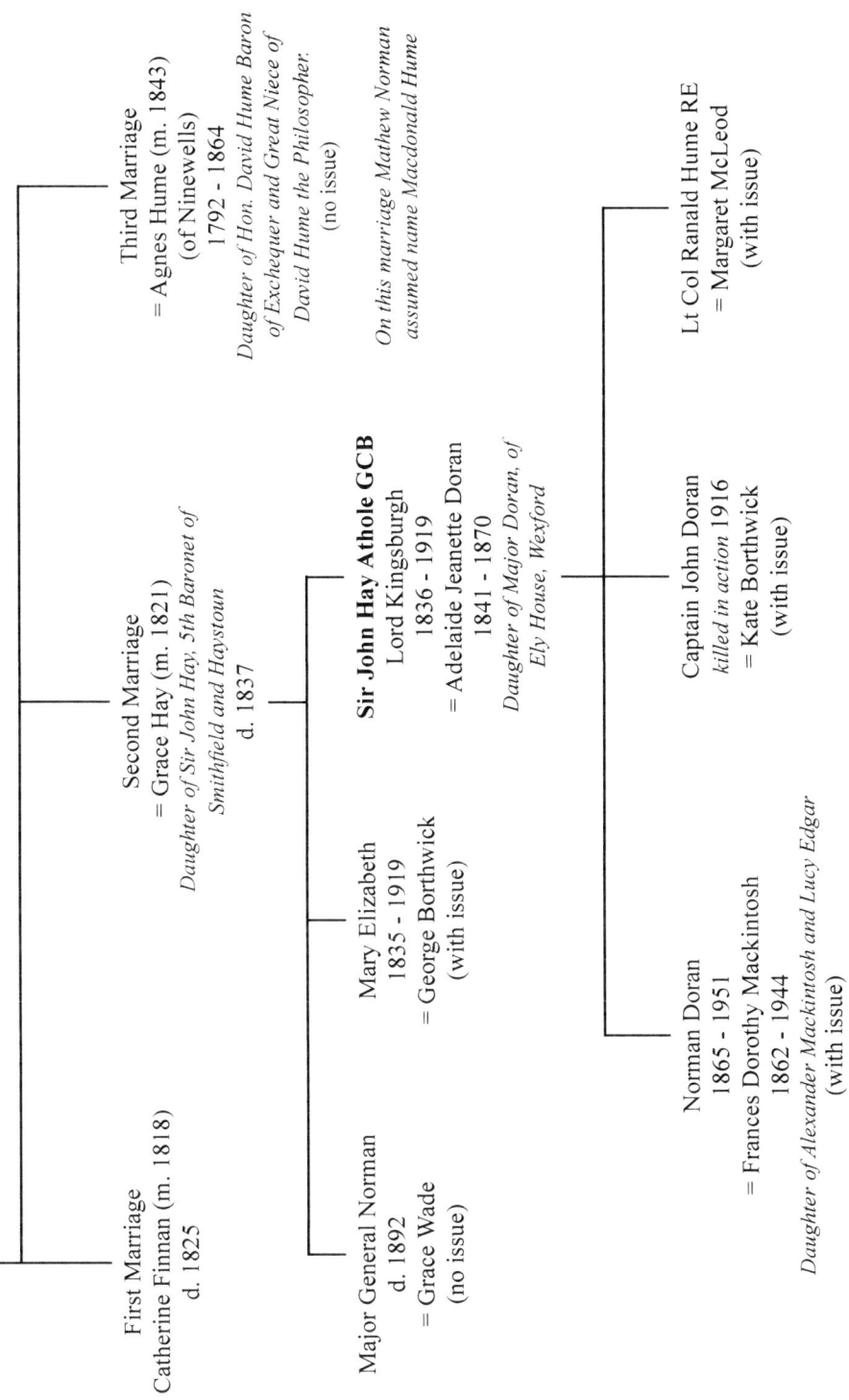

First Marriage
= Catherine Finman (m. 1818)
d. 1825

Second Marriage
= Grace Hay (m. 1821)
Daughter of Sir John Hay, 5th Baronet of
Smithfield and Haystoun
d. 1837

Third Marriage
= Agnes Hume (m. 1843)
(of Ninewells)
1792 - 1864
Daughter of Hon. David Hume Baron
of Exchequer and Great Niece of
David Hume the Philosopher.
(no issue)

On this marriage Mathew Norman
assumed name Macdonald Hume

Major General Norman
d. 1892
= Grace Wade
(no issue)

Mary Elizabeth
1835 - 1919
= George Borthwick
(with issue)

Sir John Hay Athole GCB
Lord Kingsburgh
1836 - 1919
= Adelaide Jeanette Doran
1841 - 1870
Daughter of Major Doran, of
Ely House, Wexford

Lt Col Ranald Hume RE
= Margaret McLeod
(with issue)

Captain John Doran
killed in action 1916
= Kate Borthwick
(with issue)

Norman Doran
1865 - 1951
= Frances Dorothy Mackintosh
1862 - 1944
Daughter of Alexander Mackintosh and Lucy Edgar
(with issue)

List of Illustrations

Mathew Norman Macdonald Hume WS, Sir John's father *

Lt General Sir John Macdonald, Adjutant-General
Sir John Watson Gordon.

Lt General Alexander Macdonald, Colonel-Commandant RHA
Sir John Watson Gordon

Norman Macdonald of Bernisdale and Scalpay, Skye

Agnes Hume, Sir John's step-mother *

Adelaide Jeanette Doran, Sir John's wife
Frances Truefitt
Courtesy of Lindsay Smith

Sir John aged 9 *
Robert T Ross

Sir John
Hubert von Herkomer
Courtesy of the Royal Automobile Club

Man of mark of interrogation
Charles Doyle in *Our Trip to Blunderland*

Front cover of *Our Trip to Blunderland*
Charles Doyle

Captain of Royal & Ancient Golf Club at 9th hole, St Andrews
T Hodge
Courtesy of Lindsay Smith

List of Illustrations (continued)

Sir John as Lord Advocate in House of Commons *
Cartoon by Spy in Vanity Fair.

Sir John as Lord Justice-Clerk *
Robert S Forrest

Sir John and S1
Prior to Royal Review 1905

Sir John's Funeral
The Scotsman clipping

* Photographs of original works taken by Brian Fischbacher.

I

Family History: Skye Ancestry

John Hay Athole Macdonald was born on 27th December 1836 at No 29 Great King Street, Edinburgh, the home of his parents, Mathew Norman Macdonald and Grace Hay. He was the youngest of three children.

The male descent on his father's side can be traced through the Macdonalds of Sleat, Isle of Skye, back to Hugh Macdonald (the first Chief of Sleat), and beyond. Mathew's great-great grandfather, John, son of the 9th Chief, had from the late 17th century lands at Totscor and Bernisdale in Skye. He was succeeded by his son, Norman, who married Margaret, one of twenty-three children of the Rev Donald Nicolson of Scorrybreac, Minister of Kilmuir, 12th Chief of Clan Nicolson. Their son, John, was the father of Norman Macdonald of Bernisdale and Scalpay, Mathew's father, born in 1742.

Norman lived in his younger days in Bernisdale. He became tacksman for Lord Macdonald and was granted Scalpay, a small island of twelve square miles, lying across the bay from Broadford. He built his house on Scalpay, where he and his wife Susannah lived for many years in the latter part of the 18th and beginning of the 19th centuries. Their family of sixteen children – Mathew and seven other sons and eight daughters – born over a period of twenty-four years was largely brought up there. Sarah Murray in *A Companion and Useful Guide to the Beauties of Scotland* describes being received on Scalpay in 1802 by Norman Macdonald's "amiable family with the utmost kindness, and cordiality" at their house "very pleasantly situated at the south end of the island".

John Walker in his *Report on the Hebrides* states the population of Scalpay in 1764 as eighty-four; a hundred years later it had scarcely changed. In 2001 there were only four houses including Scalpay House and eleven inhabitants on the island. Walker reckoned that the Parish of Strath, in which Scalpay lies, stretching eastwards toward the Cuillin Hills, exceeded "Lancashire, Argyllshire, and every other part of the British Isles, in Quantity of Rain", while Sinclair's *Statistical Account* of the Parish in 1795 states: "The air is moist and foggy: more rain falls in this parish than in any other part of Skye. The most prevalent distempers are rheumatism, colds, and nervous fevers". Something of their childhood environment, its ruggedness as well as its beauty, the rigours and rewards of life there, would surely remain with Mathew and his brothers and sisters all their days, wherever their lives took them.

Norman Macdonald of Bernisdale and Scalpay was a highly cultivated and well-travelled man for his time. Sir Alexander, the first Lord Macdonald, referred to him as "a man who had seen much of the world, having been in France, Italy, and America." His early travels in Europe were in the company of his cousin, Sir Alexander's elder brother Sir James Macdonald, 8th Baronet of Sleat, of whom Norman, born in 1740, was an exact contemporary and close friend. His father died when Sir James was 5, and from that age until 12 he was fostered, in accordance with the custom of the time, by Alexander Macdonald of Kingsburgh. Norman was a close friend from early days – akin to being a foster brother – and accompanied him on some of his travels. In his all too short life Sir James gained a widespread renown as a brilliant scholar and man of vision. After studying at Eton and Oxford Sir James went on the Grand Tour with, among others, Adam Smith, author of *The Wealth of Nations* and at that time Professor of Moral Philosophy at Glasgow University. He was an exceptional linguist, being fluent in as many as a dozen languages.

Sir James's always frail physique was further weakened by a shooting accident in South Uist in 1764, and the following year it was arranged that he should go to the Mediterranean, where it was hoped the warmer climate would benefit him. In the winter of 1765, accompanied by Norman Macdonald, he went to Italy; en route he met and discoursed with some of the leading philosophers and literary figures, including David Hume in Paris, Voltaire in Geneva and (accompanying him on part of his journey) Laurence Sterne in Italy. His illness seriously deteriorated, and the company proceeded via Naples to Rome, enduring much hardship on the way. In Rome Sir James suffered months of painful illness; he was visited by Papal dignitaries, and when finally failing the Pope (Clement XIII) sent an emissary each day to enquire after his health. Sir James died there in July 1766. He was 24. Norman Macdonald was with him throughout this time. Despite the religious difference the Pope ordered that he should be given a public funeral, which was described as the grandest ever accorded to a Protestant in Rome. In his will he left Norman £100. It was partly as a reward for his guardianship of Sir James that Norman was granted the Island of Scalpay by the Macdonald Chief, Sir James's younger brother.

On the death of Sir James, David Hume wrote to Adam Smith: "Were you and I together Dear Smith we should shed a tear at present for the death of poor Sir James Macdonald. We could not possibly have suffered a greater loss than in that valuable young man." His many attainments, cut short by such a youthful end, put some in mind of the adopted son of Octavius Caesar, and he was called "The Scottish Marcellus", by which name he is remembered to this day. He had schemes for the improvement of agriculture and for the expansion of employment and education, which could have brought much-needed change to Skye but were not put fully into effect (with the major exception of the setting up of a school in Portree). However, his progressive ideas must have influenced Norman Macdonald and others, leading to some of the reforms made by them. Sinclair's *Statistical Account* refers to some waste lands having lately been improved: "Mr Macdonald, tacksman of Scalpa, has given encouragement to a few families to settle on a part of his extensive farms, and this colony, from the assistance given them by that gentleman, and their own industry, are now in a thriving condition".

After his return from Rome, the only known foreign travels of Norman Macdonald were when he was sent to Newfoundland under the aegis of the government in charge of Skye emigrants.

The Kingsburgh connection came through Norman's marriage in 1770 to Susannah Macalister. She was the daughter of Ranald Macalister of Loup, Kintyre, who had the farm of Skerinish in Skye, and Anne Macdonald. Anne's father was Alexander Macdonald VI of Kingsburgh (known as "Old Kingsburgh"), and her brother was Allan Macdonald of Kingsburgh who married the famous Flora Macdonald. Old Kingsburgh played a prominent part, for which he was later imprisoned, in sheltering Bonnie Prince Charlie on his first night in Skye when he was fleeing government forces after Culloden in 1746. Anne was of the company who received the Prince at Kingsburgh House, where he spent the night, after arriving over the sea from Uist disguised as Flora Macdonald's maid. Anne served supper to the company and by all accounts, including her own, it was a lively, convivial evening. The story goes that, after leaving the house the next morning, still in female disguise, the Prince went into a wood and changed into a highland suit belonging to Anne's husband, Ranald Macalister.

Twenty-seven years later Anne gave hospitality under another roof to two other distinguished historical figures. After Ranald Macalister's death she married Lauchlan MacKinnon of Corrychatachan (a widower), a descendant of the MacKinnon Chief who at one time owned Scalpay, and it was at their house just outside Broadford in Skye that Dr Samuel Johnson and James Boswell stayed for some days and nights in September 1773 on their *Tour to the Hebrides*. From the visitors' descriptions it appears that the two travellers were pleasantly surprised by the cultured company they found there. Boswell records some of the Latin and other books in the house, which on at least one day they had plenty of time to peruse, as the stormy weather confined them to indoor pursuits (a far from unusual circumstance in those parts). They experienced in full measure the warmth of island hospitality. Anne MacKinnon, described by Boswell as "what we call in Scotland a lady-like woman", had great strength of character and humour. There is the story that she asked Johnson if he liked the Scotch broth she served: "it is fit only for pigs", he pronounced; "will you be wanting some more then?", she asked.

Anne recounted to Boswell and Johnson first-hand stories of Prince Charlie's escapades on the island and the aftermath. She also told them of scenes she had witnessed of departing emigrant ships and of the people left behind, at first utterly despairing and then resigned. These would be among the first ship-loads of Highland emigrants to set sail for North America, and in the light of the subsequent sorry history of land clearances and of the burning issue of emigration (still very much aflame in John Macdonald's time as MP and Lord Advocate), Boswell's account in his *Journal of a Tour to the Hebrides* of what he experienced at the MacKinnon house strikes a telling note:

We performed, with much activity, a dance which, I suppose,

the emigration from Skye has occasioned. They call it "America". Each of the couples, after the common involutions and evolutions, successively whirls round in a circle, till all are in motion; and the dance seems intended to show how emigration catches, till a whole neighbourhood is set afloat. Mrs MacKinnon told me, that last year when a ship sailed from Portree for America, the people on shore were almost distracted when they saw their relations go off; they lay down on the ground, tumbled, and tore the grass with their teeth. This year there was not a tear shed. The people on shore seemed to think they would soon follow. This indifference is a mortal sign for the country.

Emigration had already become an emotive issue. More than a century later, when John Macdonald was Lord Advocate and contending with the acute Highland crofting disturbances, the encouragement of "voluntary emigration" remained a key part in the government's approach to the problems of over-population and destitution in the Highlands and Islands. The people had suffered more than enough at the hands of the landowners and the powers that be, and in many parts showed active defiance against the enforcement of the law and in seeking to reclaim some of the lands wrested from their ancestors. The last step they would wish to countenance would be their removal from their homelands; only some, seeing no way of improvement to their desperate conditions, opted for a new life in the New World or in mainland Britain. Anne MacKinnon herself indicated to Boswell and Johnson that she and her family would emigrate rather than be oppressed by their landlord, Sir Alexander Macdonald, the much inferior successor to his brother, the Marcellus. Anne lived on in Skye till well into her nineties; she was still at Corry aged 95.

Norman and Susannah Macdonald had sixteen children, the first born in 1771, their last in 1794. Mathew Norman, the youngest son born in 1793, was the last but one. Norman died in 1823 aged 81, after fifty-three years of marriage. His wife Susannah, who was described as a woman "of deep and practical piety", died six years later; they are buried in the Churchyard at Kilmore by the shore overlooking the Sound of Sleat. Close by, in the Church itself, there is a monument with a moving inscription in memory of Norman's friend, Sir James

Macdonald, the Scottish Marcellus, composed by Sir James's friend from Oxford days, Lord Lyttleton.

Of Mathew's seven brothers six became soldiers; his father, Norman, was himself an early member of the Volunteers Force formed in Skye in 1803. Two of the brothers were distinguished Generals: Lt Gen Sir John Macdonald, who became Adjutant-General of the Forces, and Colonel of the 42nd (Royal Highland) Regiment (the Black Watch)[1]; and Lt Gen Alexander Macdonald, Colonel Commandant of the Royal Horse Artillery, who fought with distinction at Waterloo, where his tactics drew the admiration of Napoleon. Also, he fought in the Peninsular War, like his brother John, and he went to St Petersburg to advise the Tsar of Russia on the artillery defences before Napoleon's defeat in 1812, for which he was awarded the Order of St Anne of Russia. A third General, Archibald, became Adjutant-General in the East Indies. On his mother's side too there were strong Army connections: five of Susannah's brothers had military careers in India, including Mathew Macalister, who endured a long, harsh imprisonment at Seringapatam (India), much of the time chained to Sir David Baird ("oor Davy"). It was after this uncle that Mathew Norman was named. He did not, however, follow his brothers into the Army, as anticipated, but acting on the wishes of his father he studied for the law, and after going to Aberdeen and Glasgow universities he set up as a solicitor in Edinburgh. He became a Writer to the Signet (WS) in 1815 at the age of 22, and built up a busy practice on his own, particularly in the law courts. He did pursue his military interest as a member of the Midlothian Yeomanry, whose colours he carried on the occasion of the visit of George IV to Edinburgh in 1822. He was also a member of the Royal Company of Archers, the Royal Body Guard in Scotland.

Tall, with a fine athletic physique, Mathew enjoyed outdoor pursuits; he was a keen horseman and excellent shot. He was also a very cultured man, being exceptionally well-informed on literature and art; it was said that few men had read more than he had. Through his third marriage, to Agnes Hume, daughter of Baron David Hume (Professor of Scots Law, Edinburgh and Baron of Exchequer), he acquired the

---

[1] (See Illustrations). Another portrait of the Adjutant-General, as Colonel of the 42nd by Sir John Watson Gordon was presented to the 1st Battalion, The Black Watch in Cairo in 1893 by his grand-daughter Ethel Errington, the wife of Evelyn Baring, 1st Earl of Cromer. The portrait hangs in the Black Watch Museum, Balhousie Castle, Perth.

collection of pictures and other works of art which had belonged to her father. These included two portraits by Allan Ramsay of her grand-uncle David Hume, the philosopher and historian. One of these was donated by Agnes to the National Gallery of Scotland in 1858, and is with the Scottish National Portrait Gallery, where it has recently been joined by the second portrait.

A highly important part of his life was his membership of the Catholic Apostolic Church. He was one of the first members of the Church in Edinburgh when it was founded in 1835, based partly on the doctrines of Edward Irving; he became an "Angel" (chief pastor) of the Church, acting as a spiritual guardian. A close friend and associate was his cousin James Bridges, a fellow WS, at whose house in Edinburgh he would no doubt meet the charismatic Irving who stayed there on his visits to the capital. James's brother David, who was married to Mathew's sister Flora, was very prominent in the artistic life of Edinburgh, being secretary of the Dilettanti Society, whose members included many of the leading writers and artists of the time.

Although reserved in manner and unostentatious, Mathew enjoyed convivial company and a wide range of friends. Among these were Patrick Robertson, the "character" of the day at the Scottish Bar and later on the Bench, and Duncan McNeill of Colonsay, who did part of his legal training in the same office as Mathew and was eventually made Lord of Appeal in the House of Lords (the first Scottish judge to be appointed as such).

Mathew is referred to in a well-known Gaelic song, in which his nephew, Norman Nicolson (son of his sister Margaret and Donald, Chief of the Nicolsons of Scorrybreac), laments having been warned to give up poaching – deer-hunting in Lord Macdonald's forests in Skye – and to lay aside his gun. His lawyer uncle in Edinburgh (Mathew) wrote urging him to stop:

I got a warning from the gentry
Not to move with my gun…

Were it not for my mother's brother
The deer of the high tops would be bloodied.

The song ends:

> *From the first day I got the right to it* (his gun)
> *It was my joy and my company.*
> *I will now leave this land*
> *My mind will no more get peace in it.*
> *I will take a trip to the coasts of India*
> *So that I myself may profit there.*
> *Patrick[1] will not see me on the horizon*
> *And the loud crashing bang of my gun will not reach him.*

(Translation by Sorley MacLean)

Norman emigrated first to New Brunswick, thence to Australia. He succeeded his father as Chief of the Nicolsons of Scorrybreac.

John Macdonald inherited many of the characteristics of his father, Mathew Norman. He was very proud of his Highland heritage, and he took his judicial title, Lord Kingsburgh, from the most romantically associated place in his ancestry. His domicile throughout his life was, however, in the Lowlands.

---

[1] Patrick Macintyre, Lord Macdonald's gamekeeper.

II

Family History: Hays and Humes

Mathew, John Macdonald's father, married three times. His first wife was Catherine Finnan who was brought up in Kingston, Jamaica. She was looked after as a ward while in Scotland by the wife of Mathew's older brother, John, which is how they met. By her Mathew had four children, two of whom died young. She died after seven years of marriage in 1825. In 1831 he married Grace Hay of Haystoun, Peebles, and had three children: Norman, Mary Elizabeth (Mariella), and John Hay Athole.

Grace's family, the Hays of Smithfield and Haystoun, were descended from John Hay, 3rd Earl of Yester, and were for generations one of the principal landowning families in Peeblesshire. Their extensive estates lay in the shape of a large crescent to the east and south of Peebles on either side of the River Tweed. The family mansion of Haystoun, situated one and a half miles south of Peebles and built in 1660, is still in use, having been enlarged earlier last century. However, it was at Kingsmeadows House, built in 1795 by her father Sir John Hay, the 5th Baronet, on the south bank of the Tweed, that Grace was brought up. Sir John married Mary Elizabeth, youngest daughter of the 15th Lord Forbes and had fifteen children, eight sons and seven daughters, only one short of the Scalpay total. Grace's aunt Marjory, her mother's sister, married the 4th Duke of Atholl, hence John Macdonald's third Christian name.

Sir John Hay was described as "a fine specimen of the well-bred country gentleman, blended with the man of business". As well as carrying out much hill wood-planting and greatly enhancing his farms by making many improvements, he continued the family's paternalistic tradition in the district, and he was apprenticed with and subsequently became a partner in the banking house in Edinburgh of his brother-in-law, Sir William Forbes, which later merged with the Union Bank of Scotland. On his death in 1830 he was succeeded by his son John, who became MP for Peebleshire in 1832. He died six years later and his and Grace's brother Adam became 7th Baronet. Grace had died the year before at the age of 38, very shortly after giving birth to her son John.

Looking through the generations of Hays one finds a diverse spread of activities; in addition to farming there are lawyers (one, Andrew Hay was a WS around 1612, his son, John, a clerk of the Court of Session in 1666), soldiers, merchants, physicians, surgeons, bankers and politicians, plus one or two notable black sheep. Combined with his Highland ancestry it gave John Macdonald a richly varied heritage.

In 1843, six years after Grace's death, his father re-married. Mathew's third wife was Agnes Hume of Ninewells, Berwickshire, daughter of Baron David Hume, and grand-niece of David Hume, the philosopher and historian. Only one of Agnes's three brothers, Joseph Hume, an advocate, survived infancy, but he still died tragically young and, following the deaths of her father and elder sister, Agnes succeeded to the estate of Ninewells. As the heiress she was bound in terms of the entail in the title deeds to assume and constantly to retain and bear the surname, arms and designation of "Hume of Ninewells"; accordingly, on their marriage Mathew assumed the name Macdonald Hume. The families had been known to each other since Norman of Scalpay's day, and there was a connection between the Humes and the Hays through Agnes' brother, Joseph, who had been engaged to a sister of Grace Hay. He was a favourite of Sir Walter Scott, who wrote of him, on his death after barely one year at the Bar, as "a youth of great promise and just entering into life, who had grown up under my eye from childhood".

Agnes Hume was a woman of beauty and culture. She and Mathew set up their town house at 4 Heriot Row in the New Town area of Edinburgh, where he pursued his practice as a Writer to the Signet. They divided their time between there and Ninewells, described by Henry Drummond in *Histories of Noble British Families* as "a favourable specimen of the best Scotch lairds' houses, and situated directly above the River Whiteadder, a tributary of the Tweed."

Agnes was John Macdonald's step-mother for nineteen years, and by all accounts he was very attached to her. She died in 1864 when he was 27, just months before his marriage in December that year. Following her death, most of the household furnishings and effects at Ninewells House were sold at a sale there (conducted by Mr Dowell on 18th and 19th May 1864). As recounted in his *Life Jottings of an Old Edinburgh Citizen*, John took charge of the funeral arrangements, his father being "not strong". He gives an interesting description of the "imposing spectacles" of the funerals in his boyhood days:

The Scot who repudiated all ceremony and symbolism in his worship was ceremonious, even to the verge of pompous absurdity, in his burying of the dead. Although his church services were marked by a baldness that was extreme, when it came to burial, display was rampant and expense was lavish. I feel certain that the costs of a marriage could not compare with those of a funeral. The joyful spent little on trappings, the mourners poured out money like water. Two mutes, called in Scotland *saulies* – perhaps this was a nickname – were posted, one at each side of the house door, with broad bands on their hats, and hanging down almost to their waists. Each had a long pole, which was hung with black, looped up like a window-curtain. When the cortege was to move the saulies marched in front, and then, if the family thought much of themselves, the baton men followed two and two, to the number of six or eight, on each side, with black velvet jockey caps, and carrying great batons, thicker than a rolling-pin, black, and capped at both ends with several inches of gilding. Then followed the hearse with its four horses, each carrying a great black plume on its head, and loaded with state harness covered with silver plating, and as the hearse moved off, the horses' plumes, and the five enormous plumes above it, nodded and waved. The hearse itself was a grim black box, covered with plaited black cloth. On reaching the place of burial the sextons stood waiting with a great black velvet sheet, called a mortcloth, and this was spread over the coffin and those who bore it to the grave, the sextons having a privilege to draw fees for this ceremonial veiling. From first to last the occasion of a death was made one of ostentatious display, often in the case of persons of moderate means, involving as great a loss to the deceased's estate as follows now from the State demand for death-duties. As regards the mourners, those of the family wore bands of crape up to within an inch of the top of the hat, with great bows hanging down behind. All wore evening dress coats with white neck-cloths, and white weepers at the wrists. All these elaborate death honours were jealously upheld, and have only by degrees been broken down ... Another piece of display in connection with deaths was still observed in my boy days. It was the custom of those who thought that their position called for it, to put up a hatch-ment on the dwelling-house, and keep it there for some months after the death. It was a large square, hung diamond fashion, with the arms of the deceased painted upon it. Such a thing has not been seen in Edinburgh for nearly half a century.

His father continued to live with him at 15 Abercromby Place, the fam-ily's Edinburgh home from 1858, and he stayed there in failing health until his death in 1878 at the age of 85. Mathew suffered a decline in his usually robust health in his early fifties when, as his son recounts in his *Life Jottings*:

He got his death-sentence for heart disease from the highest in the medical profession. All that could be said was that he should support himself with port wine and brandy, and that a year might see the end. I remember his calling us round his bedside, and solemnly telling us of the warning he had received. However, having heard of the high reputation of Dr Gully, a hydropathic doctor in Malvern, he went to con-sult him and was assured that there was nothing wrong with his heart. He was put under such drastic treatment – eight-feet cold douche bath, sweating bath with plunge into cold water, etc – as would be deadly treatment to any man with serious organic heart disease. The brandy and port wine were stopped from that day.

When he returned home, he appears largely to have given up his legal practice, but, as his son writes:

> He rode his horse, and was able to do as others – attending to his affairs, joining in any amusement suitable to his age with zest, able to play foursomes at croquet, in games that lasted for many hours, up to a good old age entertaining his friends, including Lord Robertson. He lived for more than thirty years after his sentence of death, and ultimately died of pure senile decay at eighty-six *(sic)*, his heart doing its work vigorously, till the failure of the rest of his body made death inevitable. What he really had suffered from was an overstrained brain – he being a very hard worker indeed, and a terribly hasty feeder – leading to an exceptionally dyspeptic state, affecting the heart, but not so as to bring it into an organically diseased condition.

One suspects that over-indulgence in stronger liquids than Malvern water may have contributed to his earlier breakdown in health; certainly anyone who had a close personal friendship, as he had from his earliest days in Edinburgh, with Lord Patrick (always known as Peter) Robertson would not be accustomed to half measures. From the time he was called to the Bar, through his days as Dean of the Faculty of Advocates and later on the Bench, Peter Robertson was famed as a *bon viveur* and wit – a larger-than-life character of great ebullience. After his cure, Mathew did not drink wine at all on his return to Edinburgh, and Lord Robertson remarked to John's step-mother when he met her and John one day:

"Mrs Macdonald, to see your husband as he is now, would almost persuade a wine-bibber to turn water drinker;" a pause, and offering his hand: "but remember, I said '*almost*', and off he walked."

Chapter 1

Edinburgh and Earliest Memories

By the second half of the 1830s the Georgian era was drawing to a close. The 18 year old Queen Victoria came to the throne in 1837; John Macdonald's life spanned the whole of her reign and the Edwardian years that followed. He lived through the climactic events of the First World War, experiencing something of the changes wrought by them on the world he knew. His lifetime saw many changes from the old to the new, not least in the realms of the environment, transport, communications and scientific discovery, to each of which he made his own contribution, in some instances at national as well as local level. An unusual combination of attributes – an immense range of knowledge and interests, warmth of sympathies, an innovative and pragmatic outlook, and above all a fresh and independent eye for the practical solution – made him peculiarly suited to make his mark on his times. Forward-looking and never content simply to accept the status quo, the only area in which he could be termed conservative in any sense was his politics.

Edinburgh at the time of his birth had undergone the most momentous transformation of its history with the creation of the main part of the New Town; a grand design for a new style of town life, inspired by the Enlightenment. James Craig's plan for the original development – of elegant, geometric symmetry – incorporating the parallel streets of Princes Street, George Street (with its imposing Squares, Charlotte and St Andrew, at either end) and Queen Street and their interconnecting streets at right angles, had been implemented in the latter part of the 18th century. Its spaciousness and openness could not have provided a greater contrast with the cramped, closed-in disorder of the Old Town, so graphically described in the pages of Defoe, Boswell and John

Heiton. The second phase of the New Town, the northern continuation down the hill from Queen Street towards the Firth of Forth, had been started at the beginning of the 19th century. Great King Street, which formed an integral part of it, presenting a broad vista stretching for half a mile between Royal Circus to the west and Drummond Place (named after Lord Provost George Drummond, the chief instigator of the New Town plan) to the east, was completed in the 1820s. Mathew was one of the first feuars of No 29.

Expansion outwards from the centre was still largely to come. In fact, the Edinburgh of his young days remained fairly compact. In his *Life Jottings*, looking back after over seventy years, he writes:

> It may give some idea of the circumscribed character of the city when I was a child, to mention that there were country houses, still occupied, where now the city extends far out-wards. In Drummond Place there stood in the middle of the gardens the old mansion-house of Bellevue, some of the trees of the park being alive even now. The house was only removed when the tunnel between Princes Street and Scot-land Street was made for the Edinburgh, Perth, and Dundee Railway. My father remembered when a farmhouse still stood opposite where Wemyss Place is now (at the western end of what became Queen Street Gardens) ... and it is only twenty years ago (1895) that a farmhouse stood at the end of Buck-ingham Terrace.

On all sides, well within what became the city boundaries by the end of the century, stood grand houses in their own grounds. You did not have to go far from the centre to be in the country. He describes visit-ing his uncle and aunt, Mr and Mrs George Forbes (the banker) at West Coates House, which was in a wooded part, practically on the site of what is now Grosvenor Crescent: "To reach it we drove into a high-walled lane at the end of Manor Place, and on passing out of sight of the houses a shout would rise: 'Hurrah! Now we're in the country'". This would be barely two miles from his boyhood home in the heart of the New Town.

Change came gradually, and often controversially, especially where it involved an uneasy fusion or juxtaposition of the old with the new.

Right at the centre of the city, running down across the valley of the North Loch under the Castle Rock and overlooking Princes Street (which was at first entirely residential), the Mound still exhibited in the 1840s something of the hurley-burly, unplanned nature of old Edinburgh. As he recalls in *Life Jottings*:

> There were various wooden erections on its west side, including a great circular booth, of cheese-like proportions, all black with pitch, except where, in enormous white letters, it was announced to Princes Street that this abomination was the ROYAL ROTUNDA. There my infant mind was instructed in the features of the Battle of Waterloo, by a panorama, the pictures of which were probably as unlike as they could be to what actually happened on that field. Farther up the slope was a building even more disgraceful, a penny or two-penny gaff theatre, which had the distinguished name of THE VICTORIA TEMPLE, of which it is needless to say that I was never permitted to see the interior. Above this, incredible as it may seem, was a tanner's yard! At the bottom was a coach builder's wooden shed and yard, and in front stood vehicles in various stages of dilapidation and repair. A circle of stones was set on the ground, at which the hammering of tyres on to wheels was something for the boys to watch.

There was no shortage of other diversions:

> The road at that time went by the east side, over the space now occupied by the National Gallery ground. West of this there was a wide, unkempt space, which on Saturdays and holidays was the resort of low-class entertainers, who put down roulette tables, stands where darts were fired at targets by the explosion of percussion-caps in toy guns, coconut-shies, swings, tables where vendors sold what was called "Turkey Rhubarb", and cakes of chemicals by which brass could be turned into silver … Shoe-ties, penny toys, and sweets – the "gundy" and "gib" of Edinburgh – were hawked by hand, and small dogs, honestly or dishonestly come by, were offered for sale to the ladies. The air resounded with cries … A

spectacle vendor exhibited his glasses in a case, hung on the railings, and a bird dealer sold linnets in paper bags!

He refers to other degradations of "the beautiful centre of Edinburgh" proposed around that time – a two-sided street on the Mound, and the building of a south side to Princes Street (a scheme of the Town Council which was defeated only after a determined struggle) were two projects which would have irreparably ruined the city's amenity. One of the worst actual desecrations he witnessed was the laying down of the railway through the valley of the North Loch and the building of the Waverley station at its east end. For centuries the Loch, originally created as an impassable protection from the north, had lain along the valley below the Old Town and the Castle Rock. Latterly it had become little more than an unsightly, unsavoury marsh. In his *Life Jottings* he describes the valley as presenting in his boyhood days:

> A sorry sight. What might have been a beautiful sheet of natural water – the Nor' Loch – was left in a state of filth and insanitary accumulation; what in Scotland is called a "free toom", into which garbage of all kinds – old clothes, dead dogs, worried cats, etc – were thrown. A filthy marsh, it was the assembling parade of the militant boys, where class fights took place freely, and foul matter abounded, to foster the germs of disease. This may seem an exaggerated picture, but here is Lord Cockburn's account of the state of things, just before the formation of the garden was undertaken: "A fetid and festering marsh, the receptacle for skinned horses, hanged dogs, frogs, and worried cats. The presence of the water was looked upon as a nuisance, as well it might be, when the municipal eye looked at it as it was, instead of as it should be." At least it was not still used then for the ducking of fornicators, a practice introduced in the 16th century. There was even at one time a scheme for filling up the valley with spoil and rubbish, the Lord Provost of the day, when remonstrated with, giving as an unanswerable reason that it would provide ground for "building more streets"!

James Craig's plan envisaged a tree-lined canal running through the valley; less than a century later a Lord Provost proclaimed, without any dissent in the Town Council: "Nature has framed this place for a railway station", and the Waverley station was born, the railway laid down, with all the attendant furniture and paraphernalia. Macdonald wrote:

> What might have been a lovely garden, with a beautiful piece of water in it, lying in the very bosom of the city, presents now to the eye its dismal thirteen acres of dirty brown glass and its semaphore signal-posts, and has many lines of rails running along the base of the old town hill and the Castle Rock, and hideous signal and signal-boxes disfiguring the valley, per-haps the most un-aesthetic mode of laying out such a piece of ground that human perversity could devise ... a certain bronze statue of a former Lord Provost, which is supposed to adorn Princes Street, should be turned round, so that it may be compelled to face what the man it represents assisted to bring about, when he thoughtlessly accused Nature of having prepared a place for the perpetration of such a wrong to our beautiful city.

It was indeed an inspiring time – and place – to grow up in, and from his earliest days he developed a keen interest in architecture and the environment, which led him to play for many years, right up to his death, a very active part in conservation issues. For many years he was President of the Cockburn Association, the leading conservation body in Edinburgh. In the preface to *Life Jottings* he says his "most eager thought for our romantic town has been to rouse, if possible, the Jotter's fellow-citizens from a passive condition, and to stimulate in them an active interest of love of her of the matchless face – that Face which is her Fortune". It was not that he was opposed to change – far from it; he was in advance of his times in appreciating the need for progress in certain areas, most particularly that of transport. What made his contribution noteworthy was the rare combination of aes-thetic and practical considerations he brought to bear.

He was closely involved in many architectural and environmental battles, as described in his *Life Jottings* and by Lord Sands in his pa-per, *Lord Justice-Clerk Macdonald and His Edinburgh*, published in the

Juridical Review in 1923. Macdonald's address, *Incongruity and Disfigurement in Edinburgh and Elsewhere*, delivered at a meeting of the Edinburgh Architectural Association in 1907 shows the breadth and strength of his concerns on these issues. As Lord Sands remarks: "Macdonald was an enthusiast for the amenity of Edinburgh. This seemed at times almost an obsession of his mind." In his address Macdonald gives examples of incongruous new developments placed next to the old, "the most fatal" in Edinburgh being the construction of the railway in the valley between the old and new towns and building the Waverley station at the eastern end. He indulges in a dream of what could have been, looking from the North Bridge: "One can see a lovely stretch of garden reaching from St Cuthbert's to the east of Calton Hill, the Nor' Loch turned into a fine sheet of water … One can see a beautiful drive between the water and the Castle Rock, passing the Mound by a tunnel, and carried on eastwards by a boulevard road out to the front of Holyrood."

He was strongly critical of the sale by the Faculty of Advocates to the Society of Writers to the Signet of what became the magnificent Upper Hall of the Society's Library. This had occurred in 1826. In *Life Jottings* he wrote:

> Let any member of the profession inspect the splendid room and the staircase and vestibule of the Library of the Society of Writers to the Signet – the great upper room being the very finest library hall in Edinburgh – and then let him ask himself whether it was "good business" that the Faculty should sell this exceptionally fine building … and it is not difficult to guess what his answer would be.

He fought a persistent campaign against "the dreadful practice of caging up buildings with high and often ugly railings", which apart from detracting from their appearance created spaces for dumping rubbish. He instances the case of St Giles's Cathedral which he describes as "girt by a circular fence eight feet high, carried so close that here and there corners of the stonework had to be bevelled off to maintain the curve of the rail. The effect … was of an elaborate bride-cake on a round stand. The building had no base". His protests having failed to move the Church's powers-that-be, he "went round the Church one day and noted what I saw lying beside this sacred temple in accumulated dirt under the protection of the bars." He counted about seventy articles including discarded food, broken bottles and old rags, and sent a list of them to the Church Commissioners, "asking them whether these things were what they wished to protect around a house devoted to God's worship." He won the day and the railings came down. "The iron spell was broken" and down came other railings at the old university, the Royal Institution (now the Royal Scottish Academy) and elsewhere.

Much was done during his lifetime to enhance the amenity of Edinburgh, and he lists in *Life Jottings* some of the causes pursued by the Cockburn Association, including: the improvements of Princes Street; the establishment of the Arboretum at the Royal Botanic Garden, and the purchase of the ground to the south of the Arboretum to save the view of the city; the restoration of the ancient Parliament Hall in Edinburgh Castle; the removal of objectionable advertisement hoardings and prohibition of flashing advertisements.

John Macdonald's earliest clear memory was the marriage of his half-sister, Susannah, when he was less than four years old – "a drawing-room marriage", as was common in those days. He recalls the shower of silver thrown to the crowd, with the cry of "Pooer oot".

When he was five, in 1842, he went on his first railway journey. He and his sister were taken to London by their father, to stay with their uncle, Sir John Macdonald, the Adjutant-General, at his home in Bruton Street, while their father went to Madeira with their ailing half-sister, Dora. The party left Haymarket station in Edinburgh in the morning, taking more than two hours to reach Queen Street station in Glasgow.[1] They then travelled by steamer to Liverpool, and from there by train to Birmingham, where they arrived in the middle of the night, being turned out on to the line outside the station and having to walk the final stage through a tunnel. After some time they proceeded

[1] He refers to the "rather Irish" notice at Edinburgh and Glasgow stations, advising passengers to be at the station in good time, as the company could not guarantee the train might not start before the advertised time; he adds: "the failure to guarantee would rather be the other way in the twentieth century", a situation which has certainly not improved in the twenty-first.

in another train to London, arriving early in the morning, after forty-six hours travelling, "little better in time than could be done by a fast mail-coach".

In *Life Jottings* he writes of the early fears and superstitions about railroads which he heard in his childhood. They were "dangerous, injurious to health, ruinous to trade, caused all cows within reach of the railway line to refuse to be milked, and ruined the horse-breeding trade (to name but a few of the calamities which were certain to follow their introduction)." He compares the denunciation in their early days of coaches, and later, the introduction of motor transport. Many swore they would never travel by rail, as illustrated by the scene he witnessed when his father, who was in bad health, travelled to Malvern, and his stepmother, for his sake, accompanied him on the train:

> I see her still, sitting in the carriage, as we children were taking leave of her. She had a handkerchief tightly pressed to her eyes, so that she might see nothing, and begged us not to make her uncover them. A more abject picture of terror and dejection I never saw. Four years after this I went a journey with her and all the fear was gone, and she could chat and laugh like others. I remember her amusement, and that of other ladies in the compartment, when I showed her with schoolboy pride my skill in throwing sweetmeats into the air and catching them in my mouth. All feeling of looking for catastrophe was gone.

Two public events impressed him most deeply as a young child. The first was the visit of Queen Victoria to Scotland in September 1842:

> How well I remember my father taking my sister and me to a grand-stand erected in what was then a grazing field between Pitt Street and Brandon Street, and I can recall the exact location of it by having seen through the space between the floor boards, the filthy sewage-laden mill stream taken from the Water of Leith, and carried along the back of Moray Place on to Canonmills, after serving the mills at Stockbridge. Modern sanitary zeal would have forbidden the placing of a crowd

immediately above such a foul stream, on a stand in which it was to sit for many hours. Opposite the end of the stand were erected a barricade of considerable height, and ponderous gates to represent the City port of old.These were to be closed until the ceremony had been gone through of presenting Her Majesty with the silver keys of her ancient loyal town of Edinburgh had been completed. There we sat for several weary hours, until the news arrived that the entry would not be made until the following morning, and all had to go home disappointed. Next day early we were once more in the grand-stand, and full of anticipation. Everybody expected that there would be sufficient warning of the approaching procession by the sight of the Lord Provost and Council in their robes assembling, and the gates being closed. Suddenly, we saw excitement in Brandon Street – hats waved, and ladies's handkerchiefs in lively motion, and sounds of loud cheering reached us. A number of unfortunate people, who had been walking leisurely down between the crowded lines to reach their stands, were seen running back at full speed, making first to one side and then to the other, in terror of the cavalry escort that came on at a full trot, filling the whole space between the barriers, and before there was time to realise what was happening the royal carriage swept through the open gateway – no Provost, no keys, no mace, no sword being there. Quickly as they went by, I saw the Queen and Prince distinctly; she in one of the wide spread bonnets of the day, and he with a very tall hat held in his hand, both bowing first to one side and then to the other. But it was a twenty-seconds view only; most disappointing to those who had waited in vain the day before and lost the chance of seeing her well, – the carriage not being stopped at the gates, and the ceremony of the keys performed.

History tells us that there had been a failure of understanding between Sir Robert Peel, the minister in attendance, and the municipality, the latter not having been informed that Her Majesty would come up from Granton so early, the hour being about that of ordinary breakfast time. The contretemps had its amusing side, and two young ladies (Scott-Moncrieff sisters) drew up, on the same day, a clever skit, which was sung in many a street in the evening, and sold in thousands, in which the Lord Provost, Sir James Forrest, and his bailies were humorously chaffed. The few stanzas following are a specimen of the song, which is a parody on the old ditty, *Hey, Johnny Cope*. The opening lines were:

> *Hey, Jamie Forrest, are ye waukin yet?*
> *Or are yer bailies snorin' yet?*

Later followed by:

> *The frigate guns they loud did roar,*
> *But louder did the bailies snore;*
> *They thocht it was an unco bore*
> *To rise up early in the morning.*
> > *Hey, Jamie Forrest, etc.*

> *The Queen she came to Brandon Street*
> *The Provost and the keys to meet,*
> *But div ye think that she's to wait*
> *Yer waukin up in the morning.*
> > *Hey, Jamie Forrest, etc.*

All in the grand-stand were struck dumb with disappointment, and once more returned home aggrieved. Meantime, the civic dignitaries, who were leisurely getting into their carriages to come down in state, hearing with consternation that the Queen had reached the City, started off at a gallop to try to intercept the procession on its way to Dalkeith, and pay their respects on the road. They were not successful, as the cavalcade went at a smart trot, and so they came back with woebegone demeanour. The Queen, on learning what had happened, good-naturedly altered her itinerary, and devoted a day to an official entry into Edinburgh.

This took place outside the City Chambers in the High Street, and the proceedings were viewed by the young John, looking down from the roof of St Giles's.

The second event he witnessed as a young boy which left an indelible impression on him was the Disruption of the Church of Scotland in 1843, when 400 Ministers, over a third of the total number, walked out of the General Assembly of the Church of Scotland, the culmination of a long-running dispute over patronage and the right of Parliament to intervene in the affairs of the Church. The seceders, led by Thomas Chalmers, marched in a body from the meeting in George Street, Edinburgh to Tanfield, a mile or so away, and the Free Church of Scotland was formed. It was an event which, as Macdonald says, "made a great difference to Scotland in many ways". It is worth quoting his account fully, as apart from being a graphic record of the historic event, it also indicates the ecumenical slant of his later religious thinking:

> In the forenoon I had seen the Lord High Commissioner's procession, and on the same day was taken along George Street to the front of St Andrew's Church, where those who conducted me gazed up in silence – as did a crowd of others – at the gallery windows. I saw nothing but a number of bald and other heads, and wondered what was making those on the street gaze so intently. It was not my idea of a show. That afternoon I was playing with companions at home, and we were doing some children's acting, for which my cheeks were painted a strong red. Suddenly we heard a noise, and saw from the window people rushing along towards the street corner, and scenting an excitement we followed them, running as hard as our little legs could carry us. On looking up the steep street leading to George Street, we saw a long line of black moving down the hill, which as it came near proved to be the seceders who had left St Andrew's Church to proceed down to Tanfield, there to meet in a large hall. The Moderator led them, and they came on, on, on, several hundreds. It was to me a mere sight to behold, knowing nothing of its meaning; but I seem now to see before me the four-deep marchers, all in black, with white neckcloths and tall hats, and faces set and solemn. They looked absorbed, as seeing nothing of their surroundings, moving as in deep thought. My ludicrous

appearance in my fancy cap and with my painted cheeks passed unnoticed, although I was in the very front row of the lookers-on. My elder brother found me there, and whipping off the paper cap I wore, applied his handkerchief and mine to remove the clown look from my face, while still the, to me, apparently endless succession of black figures passed on. Of course it is little that I can say except to describe what I saw, but a child is quick to observe when there is passion in faces – their elders generally accustom them to that. I saw nothing of passion, rather the feeling was of sober determination of men who had made up their minds, and in whom excitement had passed away and purpose was dominant. My recollection as to what passed before me, and of the impression formed, was in complete accord with what I learned to know when I grew up, of the sacrifice these men were facing when they marched to Tanfield, giving up their homes and their living, sacrificing for the time their prospects in life. I say nothing as to the rights of the matter, of which I could have no opinion then; but it certainly was impressive to see the crowd of men, who were not deterred by dread of sacrifice from giving effect to opinions conscientiously formed and strongly held. One can imagine what a trial it was – what a sacrifice bravely shared by many a wife and child, upholding the fathers in suffering the loss of all things, so far as this world was concerned. What uncertainty there must have been as to the future, not only to those who departed, but also to those who remained! Would the great rent prove disastrous, or would both the seceders and those whom they left be able to survive and put on strength so as to present a working and efficient organisation? What fireside discussions must there have been, what hand-wringing, what uplifting of hands, what heart-searching, what demands upon the spirit of charity! Probably all who walked in that procession to Tanfield, and all who remained in St Andrew's Church as an attenuated General Assembly, have passed away. It is at least a matter for thankfulness that now, seventy years later, the bitterness of that day has exhausted itself, and that whether a real reunification is in the future or not, there is a spirit of reconciliation which enables the descendants and successors of those who took part in the long past events to meet in friendly conference. It is a maxim not to be denied that schism, from whatever cause, is an evil, which all must confess, cultivating in their hearts the desire that a way may be found to get nearer to the "good and pleasant thing", by the healing of the schisms of the Churches. But whatever may be said, the events of 1843 made it certain that the Scotsman who is looked upon as one eager and determined to acquire and hold fast – as indeed he is – is yet capable, if his conscience tells him there is a call for it, of giving up his all, as our soldier at the Alma said – "if needs be" ... What we knew as we grew up of the men who joined in that four-deep march confirmed our impression as to its character. No movement in which such men as Chalmers, Gordon, Guthrie, Cunningham, and Candlish, and Bonar, took part, and with such supporters in the laity as Moncrieff and Graham Spiers – and there must have been many like them – no such movement could be otherwise than one full of the spirit of reverent and conscientious conviction, calling for the respect of all right-thinking men, whether in sympathy with the views of the actors or not.

Chapter 2

Schools and Universities

John's first school, where he went when he was 5 or 6, was at Circus Place, very close to his home in Great King Street. There he first experienced the injustice of unfair punishment:

> I was a poor hand at writing, as I am still, and on one occasion I had to write what was called a "specimen". When it was presented to the youthful teacher he tore it up, produced his tawse (the Scottish instrument of torture for boys) and administered six strokes, well laid on. This might have been right enough – I say nothing against it. But he immediately set me down to write another specimen, and when I had done so, with eyes full of tears and fingers smarting and trembling from the whacking, he took up the torn pieces of the first specimen and compared them with the second, declaring the latter to be the worse of the two. Surely… not surprising … Again he administered the same as before to my already well-bruised hand. One learns early in life not to expect to pass through it without meeting with injustice.

He instances other occasions at school and at home when he was punished for offences he did not commit, and concludes that such treatment "may have taught one to be very sure before dealing with one's own".

His parents, as he says, "covered me with injunctions, and prevented me doing what other boys did, to keep me out of risks". This did not suit him, a naturally ebullient child. His firm view was that by the time the young child has become a boy he must be allowed some degree of liberty, and he must be taught to take care of himself. Punishment should always be measured out in just scales; it "should never be an ebullition, but a thoughtful application of discipline".

His parents' protectiveness was no doubt on account of his delicate health as a young boy. He was then "a poor creature physically" – in marked contrast to the exceptionally robust man he grew into. He suffered from "a very panting heart. Climbing a stair produced great breathlessness", and when he was about 9 he was taken away from school for a year. There must have been the fear of the heart disease from which his father was (wrongly as it turned out) diagnosed to be suffering being hereditary, and also the thought that two of his father's children by his first marriage had died young. With the possibility in mind that he might not survive, a drawing of John[1] (head and shoulders) was done in 1846; this shows the thin, delicate features of an aesthetic-looking boy, quite indistinguishable from later portraits and photographs of the man who acquired the nickname "Jumbo". His boyhood delicacy turned out to be a weakness in his growing process, and once over this he enjoyed a strong physique and uninterrupted good health for the rest of his long life.

At the age of 8 John Macdonald entered The Edinburgh Academy in Henderson Row as a Geit (first-year pupil). The brainchild of Henry (later Lord) Cockburn and Leonard Horner, the school had opened in 1824, the first Board of Directors also including Sir Walter Scott and Sir John Hay, John Macdonald's mother's father. The original rector, Archdeacon John Williams, was still there. Over-large classes were common, with the result that, as Macdonald writes:

> The smart, clever, and more studious boys formed a set by themselves, and a long string farther down constituted to him (the teacher) what the huntsman would call "a rubbishing tail" … time did not permit that one teacher should really instruct such a number, or train them for life – not the least part of the schoolmaster's province. Another evil was that each class advanced to a new course of study as a new year came round, and this under the same master, so that only those could make

[1] (See Illustrations)

the second step who had mounted and stood firm upon that
of the previous year, and the teacher only expected these to do
him any credit. Thus the start was made with a reverse handi-
cap … This tended to cause all struggle to improve to seem
hopeless, and the master being the same as before, could not
be expected to provide fresh compulsive power.

The heavy curriculum with a strong emphasis on the classics did not
help. They were rushed through Latin and on to Greek, "gaining a
loose smattering of the classics, but in nine cases out of ten receiving
no real cultivation, and remaining quite unable to appreciate the beauties of Horace or the grandeur of Homer". The first time he found
"real delight" in Horace was when he studied him in preparation
for his bar exams. "The charm of the Odes was like a revelation to
me". He is critical too of the unfitness of some masters to deal with
young boys. What was needed, he says characteristically, was "a little learning, and a little more common sense, and our ignorance would
not have made them so frantic, and they would not have inflicted
punishments which were silly". Some rein had to be given to the
element of "Puck" in any boy "who has real life in him, and an active
brain".

Scholastically then he did not do well at the Academy, disadvan-
taged also by the loss of a year early on. He left when he was only 15,
as was customary in those days; as he says, "before I learned what it
was to work". He took comfort from being able to say like Lord Cockburn: "I once sat booby at the annual examination". His only prizes
were for English reciting and reading aloud. He failed to win the main
recitation prize, being handicapped by his weak physical condition
at the time: "it was one of the few keen disappointments of my boy-
life that I could not rise to the pitch required for recitation". From
this early interest developed his strong aptitude for public speaking
and theatrical performance.

While at the Academy he had a tutor in the evening to help prepare
him for the next day's lessons. One tutor was Alexander Nicholson,
ten years his senior and at that time a student, a friend of the family (and a distant cousin). He became well-known as Sheriff Nicholson, translator of the Gaelic Bible and first recorded conqueror of the
Cuillin peak named after him – Sgurr Alasdair. He was a Skye man

himself, and was known as "The Celt". He went late to the Scottish Bar, after a highly promising career as a journalist. Macdonald writes affectionately of him:

> He was a Celt from head to toe, with a good share of pawky humour, and a considerable power of versification, both serious and comic … I think our relations at the Bar were unique. I had several times the honour of being his leader in Court proceedings. Such a thing as the pupil being senior at the Bar to his former tutor has not, I suppose, ever occurred before, and is not likely to occur again. Our friendship was cordial, and only ceased when he was carried off a good many years ago … He was a very capable man, and might have shone in literature, but his easy-going temperament militated against his attaining a marked success.

A notable contemporary with him at the Academy was William Blackwood, who for many years edited *Blackwood's Magazine,* to which Macdonald (known to Blackwood as "Jack") contributed regularly in later years. They were close, life-long friends. Another schoolfellow was Joseph Bell, who became an eminent surgeon and the model on whom Arthur Conan Doyle based Sherlock Holmes. Senior to Macdonald by three years was Henry Fleeming Jenkin, a man like him of diverse abilities, who became Professor of Engineering at London and later Edinburgh universities. He was involved in the laying of the first cable across the Atlantic and held patents for various electric appliances and other inventions. They had much in common, not least a love of play-acting. Jenkin and his wife put on theatrical productions at their house in Great Stuart Street, in which Macdonald sometimes performed. Through this he met and acted with Robert Louis Stevenson, fourteen years his junior, a protegé of Jenkin's.

Two of the most distinguished men of the century in physics and natural philosophy – James Clerk Maxwell and Peter Guthrie Tait – were also at the Academy. Macdonald did not know either of them personally, each being five years senior to him, but he got to know them later, and became a close friend and golfing companion of Tait, with whom he shared a keen interest in scientific experiment and innovation, particularly in the use of electricity.

John Macdonald maintained an active interest in the Edinburgh Academy for the rest of his life, and served as a director of the school for nearly forty years (many of them as chairman) up to his death. He was also President of the Academical (Old Boy's) Club for many years.

By the time he went to the Academy his home had moved from Great King Street to Heriot Row close by. In his free time he loved to take walks around his native city, and see as much of it as he could with his attentive eye, especially when he was old enough to go out on his own and not "on the chain" under the control of nurses and governesses. He and his companions enjoyed kite-flying on Calton Hill and skating on Duddingston and Dunsappie Lochs. Most of his holidays were spent at Ninewells in Berwickshire – "my summer home". Hunting and game-shooting never appealed to him, but he enjoyed riding, walking and other country pursuits.

In *Life Jottings* he tells of a near-fatal incident when as a boy of twelve or thirteen he was bathing in the River Whiteadder which ran directly below the house:

> I was teaching myself to swim, and had reached the stage when I could do so fairly well. But I had never been out of my depth, as where I bathed the water was only about four feet deep. Whether it was that the river had become a few inches deeper, or that there was a hole in which I had not sought bottom before, I suddenly, on trying to stand, found myself out of my depth. I sprang off the bottom, and endeavoured to shout to my brother, who was undressing on the shore, but before sound could come my mouth was full of water. Many times I jumped up, but failed to get a cry to pass my lips. At last, from the stream carrying me down a few feet, I got past the hole and found bottom, with my head above water. My brother caused an anti-climax by shouting loudly, "Well done!". He knew nothing of my agony, his notion being that I was trying how often I could bob down below the surface and come up again without stopping. During the seconds of my struggle I experienced what many have done, the drowning memory of lightning speed. A crowd of incidents of childhood rushed up from the brain deposits of the past – the nursery, the nurse, the little adventures of childhood, scenes of life of many a

sort, which no effort of intention could have brought up before me. I have often wondered in what number of seconds
all the swift-running panorama went by ... I do not believe
I could have had more than ten or a dozen plunges, and certainly each could not have occupied more than two or three
seconds of time. It was a wonderful experience, for as I never
approached to a state of insensibility, this whirl of memories
could not be attributed to anything like dreaming. An officer
has described exactly the same experience, when first under
very hot fire in the trenches.

After six years at The Edinburgh Academy, John Macdonald went to
the University of Edinburgh for one year in the autumn of 1852, when
he was still fifteen. He attended classes in mathematics, chemistry and
natural philosophy. He looked back on that university year with very
great pleasure; it nurtured his life-long preoccupation with the acquisi-
tion and application of knowledge from a wide range of subjects:

Perhaps what I learned was desultory and unsystematic, but I
have often found the benefit of it since in professional life. It is
well for a lawyer to have a good smattering of many practical
subjects. He has often to master what is intricate in natural science on short notice, and it is no small aid to him to begin his
study of the particular case with a general though not exact
and complete information. A little knowledge may be a dangerous thing, but only if it engenders conceit. It may be, and
often is, of great value to the man who knows its limitations.

This may well be very true, but it also signifies his own limitations as
a lawyer, in that his interest in the pragmatic far exceeded his capacity
for legal abstraction. His forté in court, both as advocate and judge, lay
much more in the field of criminal than civil cases.

After his year at Edinburgh University, he had the only long break
from his life in that city. He had chosen the Army as his profession, and
to prepare for the Army entrance examination he went abroad to learn
the French and German languages. Considerations of health played a
part in sending him to Switzerland. He left home in the autumn of
1853 when still not quite 17, and stayed abroad until the autumn of

1856, coming home only twice for short spells. He studied during this time mainly at the University of Basle – formative years indeed, which must have had a considerable effect on him, but of which he gives no account in his writings.

"Being abroad had done wonders for me, and I was fit for anything on my return", he writes in *Life Jottings*. He had grown into a strapping, robust six feet two inches, and he enjoyed good health for the rest of his days. The intention of a career in the Army was, however, abandoned. The Crimean War was over, and the prospects of promotion seemed poor. His uncle Sandy, the famed Artillery General, whom he greatly admired and respected, supported the decision. Also, his elder brother, Norman, was already in the service, and his father, whose health by then was not strong, wanted to have a son at home. It caused him much regret at the time. He says that had he known the Indian Mutiny was about to break out so soon, bringing the Army into active service once more, he might have held to his intention. He knew he could do well in the Army, and he records that many friends told him he ought to have joined (no doubt including some legal colleagues – the story goes that while lawyers said he made a good soldier, his soldiering colleagues said he made a good lawyer!). As it was, looking back, he says that he enjoyed through his long association with the Volunteers more soldiering and "very much more of my own way", and to a later age, than he would have done as a regular.

The Bar, then, became his chosen profession, and he began "the most strenuous work of my life", studying at Edinburgh University. His inclination was "not naturally towards close and continuous application to one class of subject", but he concentrated hard on his studies for examinations in three languages, in metaphysics, and civil law, followed by Scots law and conveyancing, all within two years. "Social engagements were declined, and amusements, except on Saturday, shunned". He did participate enthusiastically in cricket and rugby football at the Academy's new playing field, and during his year of study for the Bar exams he joined the Speculative Society, a debating society then approaching its centenary, where he did his share of "writing rather 'vealy' essays and making speeches on all sorts of subjects, with all the confidence of inexperienced youth".[1]

[1] He was very proud to be made an honorary member of the Society on the occasion of its 150th anniversary in 1914, along with Lords Kinnear and Dunedin.

Except for civil law he found the law lectures at the university "very dry"; the classes on medical jurisprudence were of special interest to him, teaching him much that was useful in his criminal practice afterwards. He regretted not having attended the classes at the College of Surgeons on that subject held by Dr (later Sir) Henry Littlejohn, for many years the City Officer of Health, who gave forensic evidence at many criminal trials, and who he came to know very well. He could not cover all the classes on offer, but typically he found time to go to the Watt Institution "to learn the practical arts of joinery and carpentering and turning, a knowledge of which has been most useful to me in many ways, professional and otherwise."

He surprised himself by passing sixth in the Scots Law exams, in a class of about one hundred, and this gave him encouragement for the next and final test – the Bar exams. At the end of 1859 he appeared before the Bar examiners at 11am attired in white tie and tailed coat, "as no other being except a waiter is expected to appear in the forenoon". He was duly admitted to the Faculty of Advocates. He was just coming up to 23 when he started out on his long career in the law, which lasted until he retired fifty-five years later.

Chapter 3

Early Years as an Advocate

From his early days John Macdonald had been a regular and keenly interested visitor to the law courts in Parliament House, "in my childhood the centre spot of Edinburgh vitality". In *Life Jottings* he describes his first visit, when aged six he was taken by his father.

> It was the sound that struck me most, resembling, as it did, on an exaggerated scale, the noise of a busy hive. No words can describe that hum of a couple of hundred people all talking at once. The floor was crowded – much more crowded than it is now – with advocates in wigs and others in tall hats, walking back and forward the whole length of the great hall, some in serious converse, and some in talk of very much the reverse character, judging by the occasional bursts of laughter. So great was the noise that when anyone wished to find a particular person, he had the services of a crier, who filled a pulpit at the lower end of the hall, and whose stentorian voice was heard from time to time, shouting above the din the name of some barrister or law-agent whom he had been asked to summon.

He was shown Lord Robertson in one of the four small courts known as the Lord Ordinary's boxes. There appeared to be nothing going on, and he had the impression that His Lordship was having a nap. He was impressed too by Lord Boyle, who as Lord President and Lord Justice-General was the premier judge. He went into the court of the Second Division, presided over by the Lord Justice-Clerk, and little thought, as he gazed at Lord Hope in his seat, that he was to occupy that chair some forty-five years later. Of these and other judges he writes: "Oh, how very, very old they looked to my young eyes! The memory helps one to realise how we on the Bench appear to the young of to-day. But I do hope that we try, and try successfully, to be more young in spirit to the young than those of an older generation were wont to be". A characteristic sentiment.

He also recounts in *Life Jottings* his first experience of the High Court of Justiciary. When still quite small he was taken to witness the trial of a man who was convicted and hanged for murdering his wife by arsenic poisoning. The forensic evidence of both Dr (afterwards Sir) Douglas Maclagan and Dr (afterwards Sir) Henry Littlejohn, both of whom in later life he knew well, made a lasting impression on him. After that the Justiciary Court held a strong fascination for him; he attended criminal trials whenever he could during the whole of his school days, and he picked up a good deal of criminal law and procedures in this way. Sentences were severe, transportation was still common: "sometimes between ten and two o'clock an aggregate of about fifty years of transportation beyond the seas would be dealt out to six or seven prisoners". In one trial he attended as a boy two young women were sentenced to seven years' transportation for the offence of stealing three or four small biscuits out of a glass jar in a little shop left unattended by its owner. The seven years' sentence was almost automatic on an offender with previous convictions.

Experiences like these fired his youthful imagination, and appealed to the love of drama and spectacle which he held all his days. It is entirely in keeping with his character and inclinations that he established his practice as an advocate mostly as a criminal defence counsel, particularly adept in jury trials, and that the book he wrote at that time was on the criminal law. No other branch of the law held anything like the same interest for him.

When in 1859 "bewigged and begowned" he joined the Faculty of Advocates and "began to tread the boards of the Parliament House", the national status of the Bar had much changed since the turn of the century. Its political influence had been on the wane, since the end of the dynastic power exercised in the country by Henry Dundas as Lord Advocate.

The Bar was also no longer the centre of learning, science and literature it had been in the days of Sir Walter Scott, Frances Jeffrey and

Henry Cockburn. In the chapter on "Our Advocates" in his delightful and witty book, *The Castes of Edinburgh*, published in 1859, John
Heiton gives an account of the Scottish Bar of a few years earlier. The
number of advocates was 462; there were peers, baronets and knights,
and twenty-five Members of Parliament. Ninety-two were authors cov-
ering many subjects:

> law, literature, political economy, politics, history, poetry, an-
> tiquities, theology, travels, novels, translations of foreign au-
> thors, criticism, and animal magnetism. Six are or have been
> editors of newspapers, and four others have been connected
> with the newspaper press. About twenty are regular or occa-
> sional contributors to the provincial press.[1]

It was still, according to Heiton, "the highest corporation in Scotland",
membership remaining as something akin to that of a Gentleman's
Club (what Macdonald describes as "a real brotherhood").

When Macdonald started out on his career, the Lord President and
Lord Justice-General (the highest ranking judge) was Lord Colonsay
(Duncan MacNeill). A close friend and exact contemporary of his father, with whom he had trained in the same law office, and later had
often been associated with in the conduct of court cases. Macdonald
describes him as:

> A model of sagacity, and one who understood men thoroughly.
> Patient, and ever courteous, one can recall his rich laugh when,
> by a few pithy questions, he had pricked the bubble of an ar-
> gument, a laugh in which it was impossible for the sufferer not
> to join. Dignified without pomposity, he was a splendid rep-
> resentative of justice, and it was well said of him in one of Al-
> exander Nicholson's clever skits, that he was: "Impatient only
> to the man, who vainly hid his hand." He was a Highlander in
> the best sense, and spoke like a Highlander. He was one who
> could not make an enemy, and who was kind to a friend.

His attributes were those which John Macdonald sought to follow.

---

[1] In his time John Macdonald was to engage in a number of these extra-legal activities, notably political and other journalism and reviews, and writing poetry and fiction.

In the Second Division of the Court, Lord Glencorse (John Inglis), the Lord Justice-Clerk, presided: "Of most commanding intellect and highly cultivated in learning, he shone in every department, as he had done at the Bar, where his most famous case was the defence of Madelaine Smith, which led to a Not Proven verdict". Macdonald acknowledges that he received much friendly kindness from him, possibly in particular at the time of the death of Macdonald's wife, Inglis having also suffered and been greatly affected by the sad loss of his wife.

The Lord Advocate, when John Macdonald entered the Faculty of Advocates, was James Moncrieff. Although a Whig he had many similarities with Macdonald, being a popular public speaker, giving many lectures and addresses, including on education, and living a very full life. He wrote many articles for the *Edinburgh Review*, just as Macdonald did later for *Blackwood's*. He was elected MP for the combined seat of Glasgow and Aberdeen universities at the first university elections ever held in Scotland in 1868 (although in that year he was Rector of Edinburgh University), and he served as MP and Lord Advocate during a period of much progress in Scotland. Moncrieff and Macdonald had a further association, as Moncrieff was the first commanding officer of the Edinburgh Volunteers, albeit more in form than in practice. Macdonald remarks rather tartly: "I cannot criticise his capacity as a commander, as during the years he held the appointment he only attended once on parade on a markedly arm-chair horse. He looked on and made a speech". Such a detached interest would not meet with the approval of Macdonald, whose military involvement was always whole-hearted.

Life in the first few years at the Bar is normally a struggle for the young advocate. John Macdonald earned his first fee of one guinea on his first morning "wearing the horse-hair", being instructed in an unopposed Teind Law matter by his friend Alexander Asher, who was then in a Solicitor's Office. (Macdonald claims that, recognising Asher's skills in debates at the Speculative Society, he persuaded him to switch to the Bar, where he had a distinguished career, and became a judge). In his first year John earned a total of £5.5s. "all in singles – as we say at cricket". He did not get into his stride until his third year; only in criminal cases in the Justiciary Court did he get any chance "of opening my mouth in argument". The criminal court and especially jury trials remained the greatest attractions to him.

The intricacies of vesting, with its destinations over, its condi-
tional institutions, its substitutions, and its subjections to de-
feasance, have never awakened any enthusiasm in my breast.
The conundrums of General Service and Special Service, etc.
etc. had no attractions for me. (*Life Jottings*)

He spent much time attending all the criminal and jury trials that he
could, interesting himself in the way cases were conducted, in the art
of examination and cross-examination of witnesses, in the application
of rules of evidence and procedures, and most of all in the close observation of "the dealing of man with man, even up to the dealing of
counsel with Judges, and of Judges with counsel". He understood the
importance of the "psychological side" of pleading, and the quality of
"pleader's tact" – the need to gauge your tribunal, judge or jury, even
your opposing Counsel, and to tailor your argument accordingly to
make it as attractive as possible. As an example of lack of "pleader's
tact" he describes in *Life Jottings* the occasion when a distinguished
counsel:

> against whom a point had been well made, and which any-
> body could see was likely to have been accepted by the jury,
> declare with an emphatic trump that "no man not fit for Morn-
> ingside (the public lunatic asylum of Edinburgh) would take
> such a view as my learned friend has pressed on you". I said
> to myself "If they happen to have taken that view already,
> telling them that they were qualified for a lunatic asylum, is
> not likely to have the effect of turning them round."

He also recommends that judges should be studied: "Frail men, they
too may be swayed against a pleader by his want of tactful mode".

The skills of cross-examination of witnesses had his particular attention; too often he saw a defence case come near to ruin through
ill-judged probing from defending counsel.

To Macdonald, then, in the furtherance of his career, knowledge
of his fellow man was as important as knowledge of law. The gaining
of this knowledge through close observation and practical experience
helped to keep him well occupied, and to ensure that he did not waste
the many free hours which a young advocate has on his hands, when

he is liable to what Stevenson called "the most arduous form of idleness" at the Parliament House. Not that there was any real danger then or at any time in his life of him slipping into such a state; for him a measure of relaxation was fine, but true rest consisted in "doing what you choose to do, but doing something – some real thing". There were many other real things that he did in those years; from the start he was increasingly involved in the Advocates Company of the Volunteer Force, as recounted in a later chapter, and to supplement his meagre earnings he undertook literary work. For many years he had closely studied the English classics, and read widely in French and German (dating back to his time in Switzerland). He had filled several commonplace books with over 1,600 excerpts, an exercise in which he took much delight, and which enabled him throughout his life to sprinkle his writings and speeches with quotations. He wrote for the press: a weekly leader in the *Edinburgh Evening Courant*, generally on a political subject, and frequent leaders and side-articles for *The Scotsman* – non-political, "as the conductors of *The Scotsman*, my good friends Russel and Findlay, did not at that time see eye to eye with me on politics". In addition, he reviewed books for the press, and wrote for magazines. Thus early, when still in his twenties, he was widening his horizons and extending the range of his accomplishments.

However, this literary output did not fully satisfy his ambitions; he wanted to do some writing more directly associated with his professional work. The answer came from advice given to him by a judge and family friend, Lord Adam, which led him to undertake the writing of a book on the criminal law of Scotland, and set him well on the way in his legal career.

Chapter 4

Criminal Law

Lord Adam told him that criminal law was one department "which the young advocate grievously neglected, doing nothing beyond defending, and often not defending well, poor people accused of crime". There was practically no instruction on this branch of the law at the universities, and the only authoritative criminal law textbook was the *Treatise on Crime* by Baron David Hume, John Macdonald's step-grandfather, first published in 1797. He needed no further persuasion. This was where his main legal interest lay and he decided to write "a practical and condensed exposition of the law brought down to date". He set to immediately, and after three years' "abundance of work" the task was completed, and in 1867 his *Practical Treatise on the Criminal Law of Scotland* was published. Dedicated to "My Brethren of the Junior Bar ... in remembrance of much personal kindness and encouragement received from them at all times and especially in the preparation of this work", it is to a considerable extent an updated version of Hume's celebrated work, of which the last edition was published forty years earlier.[1]

In the introduction to his book on criminal law, Macdonald sets out some of the main general principles and definitions which form the basis of the Scottish system. He then deals with individual crimes under

---

[1] Macdonald had another special interest in Baron Hume's work. He had inherited from his stepmother, Agnes Hume, the original manuscripts of Hume's *Lectures on the Law of Scotland* as Professor of Scots Law at Edinburgh. Hume in his will had prohibited his successors from publishing them, and over the years Macdonald had worked on transcribing them, as the originals were much confused by corrections. He found it impossible to complete this task, and in 1873 presented the manuscripts and his incomplete transcript to the Faculty of Advocates. The introductory chapter – on the nature of Scots Law and Hume's proposed treatment of the subject – is missing from the original manuscripts and is known only from Macdonald's transcript.

seventy-seven headings from theft to procuring another to commit crime; it is interesting to note some offences which are now obsolete, at least in name – stouthrief (a form of robbery), childstripping (theft from a child), stellionate (serious injury to the person), beating and cursing parents (not applicable against children up to 16), hamesucken (assault on another in his house), and leasing-making (speaking evil of the sovereign personally). Killing a judge was still an act of treason. The last half of the book covers procedures from indictment through to trial.

The book was well received by its reviewers. The *Journal of Jurisprudence* commended it as "exactly the kind of work most needed, unpretentious, clear, practical, and portable, yet bringing down the decisions to the last moment"; it had supplied the need of "a ready book of reference available in the exigencies of a practice which almost excludes previous detailed preparation, and perils character and liberty on the quickness and resources of the moment". The reviewer quotes from the "short, terse observations" on insanity in the Introduction as an illustration of Macdonald's manner of treatment. It survived through five editions as the standard work on the subject for nearly a century, and in recent times has still been referred to in the courts. As recently as 1989 Macdonald's definition of murder was quoted in the House of Lords Select Committee looking into questions relating to murder and life imprisonment.

As he was married by this point, and by the time of the book's publication he had two small boys, the "nice little sum" which he says the book brought in was particularly welcome. The publication also greatly helped to further his career at the Bar.

Macdonald married on 27th December 1864 (his 28th birthday) Adelaide Jeanette Doran, daughter of Major John Doran, of Ely House, Wexford, Ireland. She was 23, the youngest by a good many years of a family of nine children; her father was 60 when she was born, and the oldest of the children, her sister Anne, was eighteen years older than Adelaide. The Dorans (in older times O'Dorans) were an ancient Irish family, for centuries the hereditary Brehons (or legal advisers) of the MacMurroughs, the Kings of Leinster; as the judges of that province they held extensive possessions in the kingdom, including County Wexford. The family had a strong military tradition. Adelaide's father was a Major in the 18th Royal Irish Regiment. One of her brothers,

General Sir John Doran, distinguished himself in the Bengal Army: as Colonel of the 27th Punjab Infantry he served in the Afghan War of 1878 in command of the line of communications in the Khyber Pass. Another brother, Robert, served as Lieutenant and adjutant in his father's Regiment and was killed leading the charge up the steps at the storming of the Great Pagoda at Rangoon in 1852. He was 24 years old and had been called away to service just five days after his marriage.[1]

Adelaide's mother was Georgina Hughes. Her family also had a long military tradition, the first Hughes who settled in Ireland being Colonel Hughes, who came to Wexford with Cromwell's Army in 1649. Georgina's father, Robert Hughes, fought on the Loyalist side in the Irish insurrection which started in Wexford, taking part in the decisive battle of Vinegar Hill, in which John Macdonald's uncle John (later Adjutant-General) also fought. Robert Hughes was Mayor of Wexford seven times, and was made a Freeman in 1833.

Adelaide was fair of beauty, pale-complexioned with a bearing of much grace and charm. She and John would meet when she was visiting her older sister, Anne Valetta, at Edrom House, which was very close to Ninewells in the Parish of Chirnside in Berwickshire, where John spent many of his holidays in his younger days. Anne had married in 1844 Captain George Logan, who succeeded his uncle in 1849 as laird of Edrom and of Broomhouse, assuming the name Logan Home.

The marriage of John Macdonald and Adelaide took place at Ardcolm Parish Church at Castlebridge, a small mill village three miles from Wexford, the ceremony conducted according to the rites of the United Church of England and Ireland. The assistant Minister was the Rev Elgee, the brother of Lady Wilde-Speranza, Oscar Wilde's mother. The Elgees lived at the Rectory, Spawell Road, Wexford, close to the Dorans' home, in Adelaide's childhood days, and were family friends.

John and Adelaide had their home at 15 Abercromby Place, Edinburgh. The first of their three sons, Norman Doran, was born in October 1865, the second, John Doran ("Jack"), in February 1867, and the third, Ranald Hume, two years later. After only five and a half years of marriage, tragedy struck. Adelaide died at the house on 12th May 1870, giving birth to a fourth child, who survived only a few more days.

---

[1] There is a touching memorial to him in St Iberius Church, Wexford, erected by his grandfather, Robert Hughes.

She was not yet 27. No letters between them survive, and he makes no direct mention of her in any of his writings, keeping private thoughts and feelings off the page. There are but two glancing references to her in his *Life Jottings*. One refers to:

> *A gracious presence at his board presiding*
> *Doubling his pleasures, and his cares dividing.*

His will reveals that he kept all her clothes and other effects at Abercromby Place, where he lived on for nearly the next fifty years that he survived her. He bequeathed to his granddaughter, Adelaide (named after her), his late wife's dressing-case and all its contents, and "all the dresses, linen, cloaks, shawls and other things in the wardrobe in my bedroom which belonged to her".

The death of his young and adored wife was a grievous blow to him, "the great calamity of a lifetime", as he described it. No-one ever became so close to him again; a light went out that was never re-kindled. He paid visits to the Doran home in Wexford, where he always found great enjoyment responding to Irish hospitality and wit. An entry in the Ely House visitors' book in 1894 records his comment: "As jolly as ever". But her absence must have been sorely felt. Publicly he threw himself increasingly into his legal and military activities and the pursuit of his numerous other interests. Privately he was sustained above all by his religious faith and his involvement with the Catholic Apostolic Church, and by his three young sons and their welfare.

Over the years as a pleader Macdonald built up a busy practice, chiefly as defence counsel in criminal cases. He excelled at jury trials, where his penchant for the theatrical came into play. His cases in these early days covered a wide catalogue of crimes, from murder in many varieties, including a number of child murders, to fraud, house-breaking, fire-raising, theft and many others.

He writes that he certainly had more than his share of cases involving capital punishment, which he found "the most harassing and painful experience"; throughout his time as Counsel and as judge. In addition to trials for which he was retained himself, he often responded to requests from junior counsel to aid them in cases where no fees could be given. He reckons his record in all capital cases was unique. Down to the last year or so of the time when he was free to act as defence counsel, he never had a client convicted of murder, except one who was insane, and was so proved after the trial. As he writes:

> In all my other cases there was either an acquittal or a verdict of culpable homicide. But this was too much of a success to last out one's time. On two occasions in my last year or eighteen months of defence, I was called on to act for first one pair of poachers, and then another pair, for the murder of gamekeepers. There was not a vestige of defence, and the whole four died on the gallows. The spell of success was broken, and very shortly after my career on the left side of the table (the defence side in the court) came finally to an end.

This was in 1885 on his appointment as Lord Advocate.

The insanity case caused a stir at the time (1874). Archibald Miller was accused of murdering his wife in the Blythswood Club, Renfield Street, Glasgow, of which she was housekeeper, by stabbing her in the throat with a knife and striking her on the head with a clothes-beetle.

The question at the trial was not whether he had committed the crime, but whether at the time Miller was insane. Macdonald had no doubt at all about this. "The man was hopelessly mad", he writes in *Life Jottings*, and cites it as a case where anger at the brutal character of a murder caused the jury to reject the clearest evidence that the perpetrator was insane.

The jury found Miller guilty; the death penalty was therefore pronounced. There was no alternative, and in those days no appeal. As Macdonald recounts, doctors sent to examine him after the verdict were satisfied of Miller's insanity, and the sentence was not carried out.

Chapter 5

Solicitor-General

Macdonald's legal career progressed steadily. His first public appointment was as Sheriff[1] of Ross, Cromarty and Sutherland in 1874 (when he was only thirty-eight), a position he held until 1876 when he was nominated to the office of Solicitor-General, the government's second law officer in Scotland after the Lord Advocate. He held that office until the fall of Disraeli's government in 1880, when he became Sheriff of Perthshire.

Having spent most of his career at the Bar on the defence side in criminal cases, he crossed to the prosecuting side as Solicitor-General, acting for the Crown, and during his four years in that office he was closely involved in the two most famous cases of the time – the Chantrelle murder trial in 1878 and the prosecution of the directors and secretary of the City of Glasgow Bank in 1879.

The Chantrelle case attracted enormous interest from the start. It contained ingredients of mystery and scandal as intriguing as those in the trial of Dr Pritchard in 1865. Eugene Marie Chantrelle was charged with the murder of his wife, by poisoning her with opium, at their home at 81A George Street, Edinburgh. He was a Frenchman who had come to Edinburgh as a teacher at various establishments, including Newington Academy, a private school. An excellent linguist, he was described as "a man of considerable culture and polished address". He must have seemed a romantic figure – with a mellifluous name to match – to his girl pupils.

One of his pupils at Newington Academy was Elizabeth Dyer. He

---

[1] To be distinguished from sheriff-substitute as then called (now sheriff), who heard cases in the first instance. The sheriff (now sheriff principal) presided over appeals from Sheriff Court decisions and had other duties such as conducting inquiries.

seduced her, and she became pregnant. She was 15 and he 33. They married as soon as she became 16, the age of consent, in August 1868. Two months later the first of their four sons was born. The marriage was stormy from the start. He drank excessively and abused and beat her; on several occasions he turned her out of the house. He often threatened to kill her, either by shooting or using one of the poisons that he kept in the house with other medicines, which he dispensed as a quasi-doctor to various people, including fellow Masons (for he was a member of the Red Cross Knight Order), using knowledge he had acquired at medical school in France. More than once the police were called in for her protection. She was known to have sought advice regarding a divorce.

Chantrelle's immoral behaviour and sexual proclivities also caused much of the trouble. He carried on with other women and frequented local brothels, where (as revealed in statements made by some of the prostitutes precognosed for the prosecution, but not used as witnesses at the trial itself) he indulged in "very beastly" sexual practices, and was known as "the black doctor". The volume of the prosecution's precognitions runs to over 900 pages and includes many statements revealing Chantrelle's unsavoury character. One given by a woman, who was not called as a witness at the trial, told an especially sad tale. In the year before the marriage she had answered his advertisement for a housekeeper and gone to the house for an interview. Chantrelle met her there and raped her on the dining-room floor. For him the advertisement had served its purpose; she became pregnant and wrote to him, but he did not reply then, nor when she wrote again telling him of the birth of a son.

Chantrelle's dissipated ways gradually affected his work; his professional engagements fell away and he landed in serious debt. He became increasingly more abusive and threatening towards his wife, who stayed with him only because of the children, to whom she was devoted. In October 1877 he took out an insurance policy on his wife's life for £1,000, including cover against death by accident, having carefully checked what constituted accidental death in the context. Less than three months later, on the morning of the 2nd January 1878 the servant, Mary Byrne, found her unconscious in bed. She summoned Chantrelle, who after standing at the bedside, sent her away, saying that he heard the baby crying. She found it asleep, and returned to the bedroom, where she saw Chantrelle move away from the window. He asked her if she smelled gas; she replied that she did not, but soon afterwards she became aware of a distinct smell of gas in the room. This became so strong that she turned off the supply at the meter. Chantrelle fetched the doctor, who called in Dr Littlejohn, the city's medical officer, to whom Chantrelle said that there had been an escape of gas in his wife's bedroom. A fractured gas pipe was subsequently found behind a window shutter. Madame Chantrelle was removed to the Infirmary, where a thorough examination revealed symptoms indicating not gas but narcotic poisoning. She died later that afternoon, never having regained consciousness.

A post-mortem was carried out, and although it revealed no sign of narcotic poison, it confirmed that death could not have been caused by gas poisoning. No smell of gas was detected on the breath during life or the body after death. There was, though, other evidence in this connection. Both the servant and the doctor who first attended at the house had noticed vomit stains on Madame Chantrelle's bedclothes and nightdress. On analysis these stains were found to contain clear signs of the presence of opium. It was also established that Chantrelle had been the last person to see his wife, and that he had given her a piece of orange and some lemonade during the night, allegedly doctored with opium.

Chantrelle was arrested and charged with murder the day after his wife's funeral. The preparation of the prosecution case, in which Macdonald was closely involved, was intensive. Apart from the opium stains a crucial question related to the gas escape. Chantrelle denied any knowledge of the pipe, although he had been present when it was repaired some eighteen months earlier. The fracture of the pipe could not have been accidental, and there was a clear inference, from his presence at the window and the fact that there was no smell of gas initially detected by the servant, that he had deliberately damaged it himself in order to provide a false cause of death. Another circumstance, minor in itself but part of the circumstantial, damning accumulation, was that he had taken the baby from his wife's room to his own bed that night, which was not at all his usual practice. These and other facts, including the sad history of the marriage, his own bad character and vicious behaviour, his financial difficulties coupled with the taking out of the life policy, all added up to a very strong case against him.

The trial took place in May 1878, in the High Court of Justiciary in Edinburgh before the Lord Justice-Clerk (Lord Moncrieff) and a jury. The Lord Advocate (Watson) and Macdonald as Solicitor-General led the prosecution. There were originally 115 witnesses for the prosecution (of whom only forty-six were called to give evidence) and 198 productions. The prosecution steadily built up its case, principally through the evidence of Mary Byrne and the medical evidence. Macdonald conducted the examination of some of the witnesses, including police and doctors. The defence, led by John (later Lord) Trayner, had a difficult task in trying to break down the prosecution case, and could do little more than seek to show that the symptoms of death indicated gas rather than opium poisoning. Only eight witnesses gave evidence for the defence, chiefly of a medical and scientific nature. When the defence case was ended, the accused was clearly surprised that more evidence had not been led on his behalf; he asked repeatedly, "Is that all the evidence for the defence?"

Three days were taken up with the evidence. On the fourth day, the Lord Advocate and Trayner made their addresses to the jury, and after the Lord Justice-Clerk's summing-up, the jury retired to consider its verdict. A huge crowd had assembled, filling Parliament Square outside the High Court.The jury returned just over an hour later with a unanimous verdict of guilty. Macdonald then moved for sentence, and Lord Moncrieff pronounced the only one open to him – the sentence of death; in the usual form of the time it included the injunction that during the three weeks until his execution the prisoner was to be fed on bread and water only (a harsh custom which was done away with in 1888). At this point Chantrelle made an emotional, rambling outburst from the dock, before being silenced by the judge and led away.

In those days there was no right of appeal. Chantrelle prepared in prison a written statement on the case, which was included in a public petition to the Home Secretary, asking for commutation of the sentence. No reprieve was granted and Chantrelle was hanged at Calton Prison on 31st May. It was in fact the first execution there.[1]

[1] The last execution in Edinburgh had been of George Bryce, the "Ratho murderer", who was hanged in public in the Lawnmarket in 1865 – the last public hanging there. The last one in Scotland as a whole was 1869. The Capital Punishment Amendment Act 1868 provided that in future executions were to take place in private within prison walls.

John Macdonald was deeply involved in the consequences of the City of Glasgow Bank failure in a personal as well as a professional capacity. In addition to his part as Solicitor-General in the prosecution of the directors, he was himself, as he says, "a sufferer in a very serious degree" financially, due to his father's holding in the bank. The collapse of the bank in 1878 stunned the nation and had far-reaching effects. It was truthfully described "a national calamity". A contemporary account described it as:

> This great social and commercial disaster – the result of utterly reckless and dishonest speculation on the part of the Glasgow Board of Directors – an event which will long be remembered by thousands in Scotland as the saddest and darkest in their history, inasmuch as it carried ruin and desolation into happy homes in almost every town and village in the country, making bankrupts of hitherto prosperous merchants, sweeping away the provision laid up against adversity and declining strength, and depriving hundreds of widows and children of the barest necessaries of life.

The bank was established under a Contract of Partnership in 1839; as partners the shareholders did not have the protection of limited liability. John Macdonald's father held £400 stock at the time of his death in July 1878, three months before the closure of the bank.

There had been a temporary stoppage in 1857, caused by a heavy run on the bank following the collapse of the Western Bank, and this had raised some doubts about the City of Glasgow Bank's management. If the bank had been wound up at that time, when there was a deficit of £77,000 in the capital account:

> enormous suffering would have been saved ... What the bank then was it had apparently continued to be – a bank merely in name, in truth a simple channel to convey the money of depositors from the country districts to Glasgow, in order that it might be squandered in India, the Western States of America, Canada, and New Zealand.[1]

---

[1] (William Wallace, advocate, in *Trial of the City of Glasgow Bank Directors*, 1905).

However, the necessary money was made available, and the bank resumed business.

Leading up to 1878, the directors had over a number of years published what proved to be false accounts designed to conceal the true nature of much of the bank's business and the state of its finances. The balance sheets did not disclose the enormous deficits on certain bad accounts. Three of the worst of these were very closely connected in their business interests, and had a total indebtedness of over £4m. The shaky position of these accounts was well known to the directors, at least one of whom had some connection with the firms involved. To try to recoup the deficits the directors took the irregular step of investing in speculative land shares in Australia and New Zealand, again without any disclosure in the balance sheets, where they were disguised as government stock or balances in the hands of foreign correspondents. In one account the bank is described as behaving "like an insane gambler mad to be rid of his fortune". Matters did not improve, the losses steadily mounted, and the published accounts continued to deceive. The last balance sheet issued by the bank – in July 1878 – before the stoppage showed a healthy surplus at a time when their funds were in fact completely exhausted; at the same time they paid out a handsome dividend, although there was really no money to divide.

The end came as a total shock to the unsuspecting public. An official announcement that the bank was immediately closing its doors appeared in the newspapers on 2nd October. One week later the official report of the Committee of Investigation, appointed by the directors, was published. It did nothing to alleviate the prevailing sense of alarm and disbelief – quite the reverse, as it disclosed a far greater deficiency and a more blatant picture of mismanagement than anyone had expected. The total loss amounted to £6,190,983, equivalent to over £200 million in present day terms. The balance sheet (prepared by the investigators) citing this figure was in stark contrast to the one produced by the directors three months earlier. Immediately after publication of the report a warrant for the arrest of the manager (Robert Stronach), who was *ex officio* a director, the secretary (CS Leresche), and the Glasgow Board of Directors was issued. (The Glasgow Board, on which one of the Edinburgh Board – Henry Inglis, WS who was among those arrested – also sat, managed all the general affairs of the bank). They were all charged with "falsehood, fraud and wilful imposition". A further charge of theft was added, relating to bills of exchange amounting to £20,000 which they were charged with endorsing and making over before the bills became due, so that they could be credited to the bank. All the accused were committed by the sheriff for trial, and held in prison. Meanwhile the bank went into liquidation.

The law took a severe line from the start. The sheriff at an initial hearing refused to allow the release of the accused on bail (except Leresche, the secretary) on the ground that part of the offence amounted to *furtum grave* (theft of a serious kind), which under an Act of 1701 was a crime for which a capital sentence might be exacted, and therefore not bailable. A petition for bail was then presented to the High Court, but it was refused, with Lord Young the only judge dissenting.[1]

So to jail they returned, pending their trial. Their ages did not affect the bail decision – Lewis Potter, the most culpable of the directors, was 72, Robert Salmond was 74, Inglis 72, and Taylor 66; nor did their high social standing. What shocked the public most was that such an unprecedented financial disaster could have been brought about by elderly respected men who had for so long been trusted as pillars of society, commerce, and the Church.

Preparations for the prosecution of the trial itself were intense. The books and accounts of the bank had to be thoroughly gone through, the financial and organisational procedures checked, and the case painstakingly put together. This was all done, much of it by Macdonald, within three months and the jury trial opened in Edinburgh before the Lord Justice-Clerk, Lord Moncrieff, on 20th January 1879. It ended fifteen days later with the sentences of the accused. This was considered

---

[1] In his account of the trial William Wallace suggests that Lord Young's judgement was "the only one dictated solely by a consideration of the law as it stood, untrammelled by a fear of the consequences of the verdict of public opinion". He seems to have a strong point. Lord Young's opinion was that the law on this question had always been a matter of custom and discretion. By Hume's time the older custom, whereby theft with any aggravating circumstance such as the value of the thing stolen could be punishable by death, if the judge in his discretion thought fit, was dying out. "It is now dead, not to be revived, unless, indeed, we should relapse into barbarism. Theft is not, and, indeed never was capital by statute". He did not consider in any event that the facts alleged against the directors amounted to theft: "to punish any of the petitioners with death for the misappropriation of these bills would violate the custom of Scotland, as it would that of any other civilised country in the world". Eight years later through two Acts introduced by Macdonald the law relating to bail was altered – the Criminal Procedure (Scotland) Act 1887 and the Bail (Scotland) Act 1888, the latter repealing the 1701 Act and making all crimes except murder and treason bailable.

exceptionally long in those days – indeed it was then the longest criminal trial ever known in Scotland. According to Wallace it ranked, at least in the mind of the layman, as the most important. He wrote: "The startling nature of the evidence adduced by the prosecution", added to the other exceptional circumstances involved, invested the trial with an interest "which is not surpassed in the annals of our criminal jurisprudence".

The Lord Advocate (Watson) led the prosecution, concentrating on the first set of charges, which related to the issuing of false reports and balances in the years 1876-78. No evidence was led in regard to the other charges, which included the charges of theft or embezzlement on which bail had been refused, and at the close of the Crown evidence these other charges were withdrawn. Unsurprisingly, a number of defence Counsel objected to the effect of the Crown bringing charges which prevented bail being granted as a matter of right, then abandoning them when it came to the time to prove them, resulting in the accused suffering three months' needless imprisonment.

Macdonald's chief part in the trial itself was the examination of Leresche, the secretary of the bank, against whom all charges had been dropped so that he was able to give evidence. He asked him particularly about the procedures for conducting board meetings, eliciting the information that after the formal business had been dealt with he withdrew and the rest of the meeting was held in private; the directors would write up their own report of their deliberations and hand it to him as secretary for writing in the minute. The evidence also disclosed that the manager (Stronach) conducted his correspondence privately, not through Leresche, but through a private clerk who communicated directly with the manager.

It was brought out in the prosecution evidence that the actual falsifying of the balance sheets was carried out by Stronach and Potter, and that, although the other directors might not have been aware of the particular falsifications, they knew of the bad accounts involving advances totalling several million "hanging like a millstone round the neck of the concern". Despite the fact that no interest was being paid on these advances, the directors included such interest as profits, and that "interest" added up to almost all the profits declared. They must have known also of the improper land speculations entered into in a vain attempt to recoup the losses. All were parties to the publication of the false statements designed to paint a totally misleading picture of prosperity.

The various defence Counsel could not put up much of a case on the facts, but there were strong arguments on legal and technical aspects. Doubts were even expressed as to the validity of the Crown's case in strict law – whether under Scots law a crime had been committed. This was in contrast to English law where there was a statute dealing with presenting false balance sheets. The Lord Justice-Clerk stated his view quite plainly that in Scotland this class of offence supersedes the necessity of statute. At the end of the trial much turned on the line taken by the Lord Justice-Clerk in his charge to the jury. At the start he referred to "this very long, painful and important investigation ... without precedent in the history of this country", and to the suffering caused by the "great and unexampled calamity" of the bank's failure, through which "hundreds of families have been reduced ... to poverty". He was very clear and unequivocal in his summary. The mode of deception was, he said, to make the public and the shareholders and the banks "believe that the amount which the bank had out at hazard was less than in reality it was, and that their assets were better secured than in reality they were". The directors had taken the bank into areas of illegitimate banking, leading it on to the road to ruin. In his view the directors did know that the large accounts at the root of the problem were outstanding, and that their realisation was still open to question. "The conclusion that I think you will come to is that there was enough known to the Bank Board to fix the general knowledge of the position of the accounts on all the Directors[1] ... It certainly strikes one now, at the end of the day," Lord Moncrieff concluded to the jury on this score, "as not a favourable fact in this case that with the knowledge which the directors had, and the actual fact of these liabilities before them, that knowledge found no expression whatever in their balance sheet".

The jury took less than two hours to reach their unanimous verdict, finding all the accused guilty – Stronach and Potter of falsifying accounts in addition to using and uttering them, and the others of the latter charges only. In pronouncing sentence, Lord Moncrieff stated

[1] One telling proof of this was the letter from Stronach addressed to the directors in 1875, when he succeeded his brother as manager. In it he referred to the policy of "supporting several accounts of an unsatisfactory character", and asked for a committee to investigate the state of these accounts, and place on record their position, and to take action and guide him regarding them. Evidence of this letter was elicited from Leresche, the secretary, in his examination by Macdonald. Leresche said he was told to make an entry in the board minutes stating that the committee had reported they had seen these accounts put into shape.

that as the crime did not involve personal advantage, the punishment would not be so severe as if they had acted for personal ends, being short of one of penal servitude. He sentenced Stronach and Potter to eighteen months imprisonment, and the others to eight months. He indicated that if the other charges had been proceeded with and proved – theft and embezzlement – the punishment would have been very severe.

There was widespread criticism of the leniency of the sentences. *The Scotsman* referred to sentences of long terms of imprisonment or penal servitude passed on clerks and salesmen who had misappropriated their employers' money – "petty rogues" in comparison. Even taking into account the ages of the convicted directors, the seriousness of their wrongful acts over the years warranted a heavier punishment. Another comparison was made with a bank manager who got six years' penal servitude for an offence which caused "not the thousandth or rather the millionth part of the misery" caused by the City of Glasgow Bank Directors. *The Glasgow Herald* said it could not take the same lenient view as the Lord Justice-Clerk of the conduct of the directors so far as relating to their own personal advantage; they all had the strongest personal interest in keeping the bank afloat, and they could only do so by falsifying the balance sheet. They were all men of high repute in the commercial and religious circles of Glasgow, honoured and looked up to as magnates in the Church and on the Exchange. They knew that if they had issued a proper balance sheet showing the true state of affairs they would have been dishonoured and lost their fortunes in the general collapse of the bank. *The Herald* concluded nevertheless that "looking at all the circumstances, we cannot say ... that the sentences ... are inadequate to the offence". It was almost alone in this view.

Further revelations of earlier misdoings in the bank's affairs came to light three years later when James Nicol Fleming, a director until 1875, was finally brought to trial. Fleming had been insolvent since 1871, but during his time as a director of the bank he continually increased his indebtedness to the bank, which was never met. He got unsecured advances for his business amounting to over £1m. When the bank stopped he fled the country, and it was not until his return in 1882 that he was arrested and charged with fraud, and embezzling over £600,000, and "being conscious of your guilt ... did abscond and flee from justice". As with the other trial, only the charge of using and uttering false reports and accounts was pursued. Fleming pleaded guilty to this and was sentenced by Lord Moncrieff to eight months imprisonment. He got off lightly – perhaps due to his suffering, not surprisingly, from "nervous prostration".

John Macdonald's personal financial loss from the collapse of the bank was very serious. His father died three months before the closure of the bank, owning four shares (£400 stock) in it; John being entitled to one-third of the residue of his father's estate stood to lose the major part – conceivably all – of that inheritance. This was because of the unlimited liability of the shareholders for the bank's debts, and the fact that the wealthier shareholders had to meet the calls for payment made against the large number of those unable to pay the first call, and similarly with subsequent calls. Uncertainty was all.[1]

In the event there were two calls on shareholders – the first for £500 per £100 stock, and the second £2,250 – making a total of £11,000 paid out of the estate of his father. (In present-day terms this would amount at the very least to £350,000). The estate was able to meet this liability in full, but at the time there was the great concern that more calls could follow. As Macdonald writes in *Life Jottings*:

> It was an awful time. It will give an idea of the sweeping character of the calamity to mention that after the last call, out of all the many shareholders of the luckless bank, there were only sixteen people or sets of people left standing, and able to pay more if called on.

Even these would have been "brought to penury" if an Assets Company had not been formed to acquire the assets of the bank, enabling the liquidation to be brought to an end. In the whole liquidation nearly £6m was received from contributories.

Macdonald's plight was bad enough, but it could have been even worse. As one of the executors under his father's will, he could have been held personally liable. The decision in a test case (Muir) was that trustees on the City of Glasgow Bank register were personally liable for the

---

[1] The gravity of the situation can be gauged by what happened to the Caledonian Banking Company of Inverness. As a result of its holding £400 of City of Glasgow stock – the same amount as Macdonald's father – it was forced into liquidation, and as much as £150,000 was set aside to meet its possible liability in the Glasgow Bank liquidation.

debts of the bank, on the basis that once registered as owners of the shares they assumed the rights and liabilities of partners in the bank as laid down in the Contract of Partnership. The extraordinary result was that every trustee could be liable to his last penny.[1] This applied equally to executors, although in their case the shares would have to be registered in their name purely as an administrative requirement before they could be transferred to the beneficiaries.

Macdonald's position had a special peculiarity that enabled him, after much litigation, to avoid the direst possible consequences. After his father's death in July 1878, the confirmation in favour of his executors was sent to the secretary of the bank requesting the transfer of the stock from the name of the deceased into the names of the executors. An entry was made by a clerk in the Register of Transfers, but not in the Register of Members. It was not until after the stoppage of the bank in early October that another clerk entered the executors in the Register of Members. On the liquidation of the bank the executors were listed as contributories in their own right and so personally liable. Macdonald and his co-executors petitioned the Court of Session to have this changed, and their names included only in their representative capacity. The court granted this, holding that the entry on the Register of Members, having been made after the stoppage of the bank, was unwarranted and could receive no effect. The liquidators appealed to the House of Lords against this decision and a compromise settlement between the parties was announced, under which the executors' names were to be removed from the list of contributories in their own right and included as contributories representative of others. The executors were to pay the liquidators £500, with neither party having any further claim for costs. The Appeal Court (House of Lords) accepted this arrangement, subject to the sanction of the Court of Session, which was granted.

So ended the legal saga for Macdonald, although not the financial worries. Other cases continued; between 1879 and 1882 there are forty-eight reported cases against the liquidators of the bank, raised by trustees, curators and others. They met with varying results. It was not until October 1882 that the liquidation closed and he was "set free", as he put it in a letter to William Blackwood.

[1] Lord Deas said in the Court of Session that in his twenty-five years on the Bench it (the Muir case) was the most painful judgement he had given. On appeal to the House of Lords the decision was upheld.

Chapter 6

Law, Politics and Literature

During his four years as Solicitor-General, from 1876 to 1880, Macdonald's earnings decreased considerably, adding to the financial instability he suffered as a result of the City of Glasgow Bank disaster. The office brought nothing of value, he wrote in *Life Jottings*:

> except the honour of the position, the emoluments not reaching to a thousand a year. In my case the possession of the post involved on more than one occasion a loss greater than the official salary. When the trial of the City of Glasgow Bank Directors took place, private practice fell off to nothing, as it was known that close attendance would have to be given to a long trial, and of course as practice was stopped, it took a considerable time before new work came in.

The same thing happened with the Chantrelle case. In addition, he had the expense of standing for Parliament, as was expected of the Solicitor-General. He had first stood in 1874 as Conservative candidate in the City of Edinburgh against Duncan McLaren, a radical Liberal and highly respected Lord Provost, who did much for the improvement of Edinburgh. He stood against him again in 1880, each time polling little more than a third of the number of votes that McLaren did. These heavy defeats did not alter Macdonald's regard for his victor, who he describes as delivering Edinburgh from the "Slough of Despond" into which she had fallen. "He had brains in abundance, and he used them unsparingly for his city."

In between these two elections Macdonald stood in 1879 in the Haddington Burghs, where the Conservative cause was as hopeless as in the city; at one meeting in Haddington he was howled down and could not continue. His conduct in fighting spirited campaigns was remarked upon, but he must have welcomed some years later the calmer waters of the constituency of Edinburgh and St Andrews universities for which he was elected in 1885.

Macdonald continued to write articles and give addresses on an increasing variety of subjects – political, legal, military, educational, scientific, which helped to supplement his earnings. In 1877 he ventured into fiction when *Blackwood's* published his story for children, *Our Trip to Blunderland or Grand Excursion to Blundertown and Back*, written under the thinly disguised pseudonym of "Jean Jambon" (John Ham) and illustrated by Charles Doyle, "my friend", the author calls him. It grew out of his story-telling in the nursery to his three sons, Norman, John (Jack), and Ranald. The preface begins:

> The nursery has its share of my day, in such fashion that little people may not think big people created to stop fun and to be a throttle-valve on animal spirits. But there are romps and romps, some being beyond an adipose six-foot-two. Hence this story. Perhaps it will prove acceptable at cooling times in other nurseries, as it was in ours.

The story is an Alice in Wonderland type tale, recounting the fanciful journey and adventures of "three little boys (whose names you must not know – so choosing something like them, they shall be called Noval, Jaques and Ranulf)". The debt to Lewis Carroll is acknowledged in the Preface in typically punning fashion, the reference to Alice appearing in the story provoking one of the most contrived puns: "It may be thought that in introducing a certain little Lady ALICEnce has been taken". The book itself has an abundance of word-play and of comical characters and strange adventures – the sort of mixture much loved by young children. He places the three boys in normal situations, such as in a school and a court of law (where they appear as "puny Judges") and on various forms of transport; all are made the reverse of real. Likewise the characters, the "whys man" for example "... the queerist man that ever was seen", who inspires one of Charles Doyle's wittiest drawings. "Nobody could fail to see that he was a man of mark of interrogation, for when you looked at him you saw a great deal of curl at the head, and when you reached his feet he came to a stop".[1] It all, not surprisingly, turns out to be a dream:

> ... and Ranulf awoke to the fact that he had been dreaming. But although he has returned from Blunderland, leaving behind his long nose, he has brought a pretty long tail home with him instead of it; and now, as he was often taught never to be a tale-bearer, it has been carried to the Black woods, and hid away in these leaves, in the hope that it may amuse other little people who chance to unfold it.

The story shows how easily he entered the world of childhood. In addition to his story-telling he entertained children with his skills as a mimic, a singer of comic songs, and a juggler and conjurer (he could palm a billiard ball in his large hand). He was an enthusiastic actor: both he and Adelaide took part in amateur theatricals. Mostly he maintains in the book a light touch (if you allow that the often laboured punning would pass with the young), but once or twice he cannot resist drawing a moral, as when he adds a footnote after the audience at the concert the boys attend in Blundertown shout:

> "No, no! No Wagner, please; we don't want the music of the future; no promissory notes for us" ... Boys should take this as one of their mottos – "No bills or promissory notes for us". There are too many sharps ready to press them on young naturals and flats, and they very often end in harsh keys and gloomy bars.

He took a close interest in how the book was to be presented; writing to his friend William Blackwood, he says:

> I do not concur with the "professionals", as I think the eccentricity of the title page is a recommendation. I am decidedly against putting an elaborate fictional title opposite the frontispiece. The enclosed title will do well, if the ticket is brought down about ¼ of an inch, and the words above wider set from

---

[1] (See Illustrations)

one another. Also the woodcut should be placed with the <u>cen-tre of the ticket</u> in the centre of the page, and not the centre measured from the outside of the little figures. With these changes I think it will be quite satisfactory.

Blunderland was a considerable success, running quickly into a second edition. According to Rodney Engen in his biography of Richard Doyle, Charles's brother, it sold 15,000 copies in a year; its popularity was greatly enhanced by the sixty delightful illustrations by the artist Charles Doyle (twenty full-page and forty vignettes), which exactly match the childish whimsy of the story. Author and illustrator were friends: an unusual pair on the face of it – the successful lawyer and public figure, and the unworldly, unstable draughtsman and artist.

Doyle was the father of Arthur Conan Doyle (and nine other children) He was one of the well-known Irish family of caricaturists and artists; his father was John ("HB"), and his brother Richard ("Dicky") Doyle of *Punch* fame. His work is in similar style. His line drawings and depiction of the world of fantasy were especially suited to book illustration. Among many others he illustrated editions of *Travels of Mungo Park in Africa*, *Robinson Crusoe* and *Pilgrim's Progress*. He also did the first published drawings of Sherlock Holmes in *A Study of Scarlet*. Charles was sent to Edinburgh at the age of 17 to work as a draughtsman in the Scottish Office of Works under Robert Matheson, the Chief Surveyor for Scotland, where he remained, at almost the same meagre salary, all his working days. He suffered severely from depression and had to retire at the age of 44; he spent his last years in a mental asylum, his health broken by melancholia and alcoholism, and he died in 1893.

A later cheap edition of *Blunderland* failed. Macdonald wrote to Blackwood in October 1881:

My Dear Bill,

Many thanks for cheque. I feel I ought not to keep it, as from a communication I got from your business department, I find I am due you a big sum owing to the cheap editions of Blunderland having fallen flat. I am afraid I did not devote any energy to pushing them myself, and that the change in your headman just at the time, was not favourable, as our old friend took such an interest in it. However *n'importe*. Only I am rather light just at present but I hear we are to get set free by the liquidators (of the City of Glasgow Bank) very soon, when I shall be able to square up.

Thine ever,

He did not venture into fiction again until a serial story was published in *Chambers's Journal* in 1909, when he was over 70.

William Blackwood was a close friend from school days. They had many interests in common: they were golfing companions and shared the same political Conservative views. Blackwood asked him to contribute to *Maga*, as *Blackwood's Magazine* was commonly called. This he did over a period of twenty years, starting in 1879 when Blackwood became editor, a position he held until his death in 1912. Macdonald's articles were mostly on political subjects; they all appeared anonymously, as was the usual custom of the *Magazine* – and his own wish. The first, *Political Rabies*, in December 1879, attacked "the present rabid style of Liberal platform declamation". It is pretty weighty stuff. The second, entitled *The Stump Ministry: Its First Session*, appeared in the October 1880 issue, after the first few months of the Gladstone government, which had been elected with an overwhelming majority. He portrays the Liberals' "stump agitation" as appealing by unscrupulous means to men's passions, in contrast to the more principled ways of his own party. This was how Gladstone had won power.

> The party that does not appeal to the passions of men – that neither rouses their natural propensity to destructiveness, nor offers bribes to their selfishness – can least afford to leave the household suffrage voter uncared for, in the fond hope that his action at the ballot-box will be guided by sound principles.

With Disraeli's fall in 1880, Macdonald's term as Solicitor-General ended. He took silk, became Sheriff of Perthshire, and returned to private practice at the Bar. In 1882 his fellow advocates elected him Dean of the Faculty of Advocates; beating two others by a considerable majority.

In October 1882 he led the defence in an unusual case which

attracted enormous publicity. It involved a crime – violation of a grave and body-snatching – which had not occurred since the days of Burke and Hare half a century before. In this case the motive was different from selling bodies to medical schools for dissection; it was the hope of getting a reward for the return of the body. As the body was the embalmed one of Lord Crawford, 25th Earl of Crawford and 8th of Balcarres, the case caused something of a sensation. The burial had taken place in the family vault at Dunecht House, Aberdeenshire, in December 1880, but it was not until the following December that the vault was found to have been tampered with and the body removed from its coffin. Previously the only sign had been in May 1881 when an odour as of stale flowers, or of *arbor vitae*, was detected coming through a crevice which had been filled up on the outside of the vault. The discovery of the removal of the body had not been made at that time, so whoever perpetrated the crime had deliberately gone back into the vault and moved a slab to draw attention to the situation. Suspicion fell on Charles Soutar, an ex-mole catcher on the Dunecht estate, who had been sacked for persistent poaching, and he was brought to trial for violating a sepulchre (*Crimen Violati Sepulchri*), concealment of a dead body, and attempting to extort a reward.

The case against Soutar was almost entirely circumstantial. He had just finished a prison sentence for poaching on the estate and was known to have been in the neighbourhood two days before the peculiar smell from the mausoleum was noticed; he dropped hints locally about the mysterious disappearance or murder of someone, and claimed he had come across a gang of four masked and armed men in the Echt woods late one night, who had buried a body there. He wrote an anonymous letter to the estate land agent openly stating that the body had been removed from the vault, but this was regarded as a hoax and not acted on. He offered to bring matters to light, including disclosure of the place where the body had been concealed, allegedly so that he could claim a reward. Macdonald referred in his address to the jury to the almost total lack of direct evidence, and the fact that the crime was one which could not physically have been committed by one man alone, yet, although others had been arrested, no one else was tried. He drew applause from the body of the court on two occasions in his address – not an unusual happening with him. The second time was at the end of the trial, when he said he was convinced that if the

Lord Advocate and Solicitor-General had nobody pulling at their coat-tails, the case would never have been presented to a jury, and the jury would not have been misled by the attempt to give a criminal finish to this sensational case by the arguments which the Solicitor-General had addressed to them. The next day he informed the court he had received a letter, and he wished to intimate that he had not intended to insinuate in his address that the judge, Lord Craighill, had influenced the prosecution.

The jury returned a unanimous verdict of guilty. Lord Craighill imposed a sentence of five years' penal servitude – the sentence perhaps more severe than if the body had been that of a mortal of lower standing.

In the following year Macdonald led the defence in another case which excited much interest and controversy – the trial of the "Strome Ferry Rioters". Although not concerned with the Highland crofting disturbances, which had already led to the setting up of the 1883 Napier Commission, it was a further sign of Highlanders trying to preserve part of their heritage, which they saw as threatened by outsiders, and going to the length of taking the law into their own hands where they felt this to be justified. As it involved what they considered to be Sabbath desecration – to this day an emotive subject in parts of the Highlands and Islands – feelings ran high. The case of mobbing and rioting was brought against Alexander Gollan and nine other men in the High Court in Edinburgh before Lord Justice-Clerk Moncrieff. The charge was that, armed with staves, sticks, bludgeons or other weapons, they assembled with a crowd at Strome Ferry pier, taking possession of it for twenty-four hours, with the aim of ("riotously and tumultuously", as the indictment put it) preventing the unloading on a Sunday of fish from steamboats and their transmission by rail. In attempting to break up the crowd various policemen, including the chief constables of Ross and Cromarty and of Sutherland, were assaulted, and the police were unable to carry out their instructions.

Macdonald in his address to the jury spoke with feeling about the religious belief behind the men's action. A deeply religious man himself, albeit of a different persuasion from the Free Church of Scotland, he clearly felt their position keenly. He said that the actions of the accused arose "out of a belief that the law which they had been taught at their mothers' knee was being outraged from week to week by those who had come there and did not belong to the district at all". The whole community felt this. Any of the jury who knew the Highlands well knew that:

> The line of tradition which came down to them from old times remained much longer operating upon the hearts and the disposition of the minds of men in these and outlying and unsophisticated districts than in the districts in which the jury and most of them dwelt, in which modern civilisation was perhaps doing a great deal of good in one way, but in some other ways might be doing a great deal of harm ... Men such as these prisoners looked upon this outrage upon their feelings as not being one directed against them but directed against a much higher law – one handed down not merely from their fathers, but from the earliest times, under Divine precept.

He contended that two old statutes were still in force in Scotland, prohibiting the carrying on of ordinary business on the Lord's Day, and these people "saw the officers of the law not only not interfering to prevent the traffic themselves, but lending their hands and giving sanction to it". He concluded:

> The whole matter might have been settled by the exercise of a little common sense, and could have been settled by a civil process. To call the people a riotous and evil-disposed mob, desiring to put the lieges in danger of their lives, was an absolute abuse of terms.

He drew applause at the end of his address, and at other stages, from a large attendance at the trial, which included three eminent Free Church ministers.

The Lord Justice-Clerk (Moncrieff) in his summing-up said that whatever the merits of "the very important questions" raised by Macdonald, no man was entitled to take the law into his own hands, or to resist officers of law; the only question the jury had to consider was whether the accused had any such right in this case. The jury unanimously found them guilty of mobbing and rioting but recommended the prisoners to the utmost leniency of the court "on account of their ignorance of the law and the strong religious convictions they hold against Sabbath desecration". The judge imposed sentences of four months' imprisonment on the men, which provoked immediate strong reaction led by the most prominent Ministers of the Free Church. Highly unusually, the jury held a meeting on the day following the verdict, at which they stated their unanimous view that the sentences were too severe in the circumstances of the case, and the great majority of them supported the Ministers' proposal to send a petition to the Home Secretary asking for mitigation. This was sent, questions were put in the House of Commons, and after two months in jail the prisoners were released.

The case and its aftermath present a bitter foretaste of the conflicts arising from the Crofters' trials soon to follow. Feelings ran high in the press and among the public. *The Scotsman* newspaper used intemperate language in condemning the "Rioters", and more especially the Free Church Ministers, who it maintained were the true guilty men:

> The spirit which actuates the Free Church Presbytery of Loch Carron to call for prohibition of Sunday trains in their blessed district by the strong arm of the law, and which causes the rioters of Strome Ferry as vindicators, against a wicked world, of the law of Scotland and that of God, is essentially the spirit of intolerance and tyranny … their whole conceptions of life and humanity are grotesque.

Chapter 7

The Crofting Disturbances

Macdonald stood unsuccessfully as a Conservative candidate three times in Parliamentary elections – in 1874 and 1880 in the City of Edinburgh against Duncan McLaren, the radical Liberal, dubbed "the Member for Scotland", and in 1879 in the Haddington Burghs. In a lengthy address to the Conservative Association of Glasgow in December 1874 on *The Strength of Our Position and How to Use It* (published by Blackwood) he set out his political beliefs. The Conservatives had earlier in the year won an election, ending forty years of Liberal rule. He thought their strength lay in their occupying the higher moral ground of principle in comparison with the Liberal party, which was opportunistic, extremist, and made up of many "isms" and sects such as Ultramontane Romanism, Evangelical Dissent, Quakerism, Secularism, Atheism, Radicalism, and Red Republicanism. He had a rooted dislike of Gladstone with his "demagoguism" and "sensation politics". The Conservative party by contrast had "no need to truckle to cliques, or to coquette with revolutionists".

A strong factor in much of this came no doubt from his religious faith. Established religion was under severe threat, and he saw Britain as standing:

> between the devil and the deep blue sea – the devil of the wildest communism and the deep raging sea of religious discord, revolution in the State, further dissolution in the Church. And who will say that there is no danger of Rome … making one last bid for power by throwing in her lot with Revolution on the large scale, as she has done under our very eyes on the small scale in Ireland?

The weighty speech is leavened throughout in typical style by quotations and references from a range of sources, including Thomas Moore, Milton, Bunyan, Swift, and Shakespeare.

John Macdonald was appointed Lord Advocate when the Conservatives were elected in July 1885 and Lord Salisbury succeeded Gladstone as Prime Minister. His election as MP for Edinburgh and St Andrews universities[1] followed in November. He remained Lord Advocate until October 1888 apart from an interval of six months in 1886 when Gladstone's government was returned to power.

The main function of the Lord Advocate (originally known as the King's Advocate) was then, and still remains, that of principal law officer of the Crown in Scotland, responsible for the prosecution of criminal cases and advising on Scottish legal affairs. In more recent times he had become a much more powerful figure politically, especially in the person of Henry Dundas, operating virtually as the manager of Scottish affairs. There was much resentment at this concentration of power in one man, and with the increasing feeling over years – decades – that Scottish business was inadequately dealt with at Westminster, there was strong support for the restoration of the office of Secretary for Scotland, which had been abolished at the time of the 1745 rising. A Bill to restore the office had been introduced in 1885 by the Earl of Rosebery on behalf of the Liberals. Salisbury's government re-introduced the Bill, which was passed in August of that year. The Duke of Richmond and Gordon became Secretary for Scotland and the Scottish Office was set up.

Macdonald's chief contribution to the establishment of the new order was to secure the use of Dover House in Whitehall for the Scottish Office. A handsome town residence built in the 1750s it had been at one time the home of Lady Caroline Lamb and was often visited by Lord Byron. Latterly Lord Dover, the chief benefactor towards the building

---

[1] This constituency and one combining Glasgow and Aberdeen universities were set up under The Representation of People Act 1868 and gave members of the university courts and general councils and graduates of the universities a right to vote (by post) which was additional to their normal vote in the constituency where they resided. The Representation of People Act 1918 introduced a new system of three Members representing all four Scottish universities – these included most notably John Buchan in the 1920s. The seats, in England and Scotland, were abolished in 1948. Macdonald was the second Member for Edinburgh and St Andrews, succeeding Dr Lyon Playfair (later Lord Playfair, a Liberal). The constituency work was much less arduous than for other MPs.

of the National Gallery in Trafalgar Square, had resided there. How Macdonald, travelling by train with Lord Salisbury, persuaded the PM then and there that the property should be made over to the Scottish Office makes an interesting story. In a letter to *The Scotsman* on 13th May 1919, following Macdonald's death, Sir Henry Craik, a high-ranking Civil Servant and at one time MP for Glasgow and Aberdeen universities, describes what happened:

> When the organisation of the office was in its earliest stage, I was the only permanent official in charge. The question of its situation was naturally the subject of constant talk between the Lord Advocate and myself, and on one occasion I suggested – not, I confess, with much hope of success – that we should try for Dover House, which was then a much coveted object to many larger Departments. The Lord Advocate was not daunted by the difficulties which I foresaw; and the same evening in the House he tackled Sir David Plunket – then First Commissioner of Works – on the subject, and boldly advanced his claim. It was met, he told me, by a burst of laughter at such audacity, and by the objection that Dover House was to be assigned as a residence for the Prime Minister; but Sir David was good enough to suggest, as an admirable substitute, twelve vacant rooms above the newly-erected Post Office in Bedford Street, Covent Garden! This rebuff was taken with characteristic good humour by Macdonald, but had no effect whatever in discouraging his enterprise; and he soon afterwards found his opportunity. Almost the next day, it fell out that Macdonald travelled to Osborne in the company of Lord Salisbury and Sir Charles Lennox Peel, the Clerk of the Council, to be sworn of the Privy Council. On his return he came straight to my room in the highest spirits to tell me the story of his achievement. On the journey conversation chanced to turn on the newly-born office, and Lord Salisbury asked as to the progress of the infant. Macdonald gave the rosiest account, except that they were denied the house which they thought desirable and necessary. "What is that?" asked Lord Salisbury. "Dover House", said Macdonald, "but I have been laughed at, and told it was required for you". "For me!"

answered Lord Salisbury, "I have a house already, and I have
no thought of interfering with Dover House, or with your
claim to it". "Would you mind putting that on paper?" asked
Macdonald; and to this the Premier readily agreed. Macdonald brought back with him a paper which had been submitted
to Lord Salisbury at Osborne, and signed by him, which ran
very nearly in words like these (I quote from memory): "I
consider that for the success of the Scottish Office a suitable
home is essential, and I think that Dover House might with
great advantage be assigned for the purpose". He enclosed
the Premier's order to Sir David Plunket, congratulating him
on being able to retain the twelve rooms over the Post Office
for some suitable object, and he recommended to me to lose
no time in giving a sign of occupation by transferring some
loads of records. That recommendation was carried out without an hour's delay, and the tenancy thus begun was never
broken or even threatened, in spite of the jealousy which it
aroused in many quarters.

Writing to the Duke of Richmond and Gordon on 20th August 1885,
Salisbury takes a light-hearted view:

> ... I signed away Dover House for you to reside in. I believe I
> have as much right to sign away Westminster Abbey – but the
> Lord Advocate seemed to take it very easy. No doubt the free-
> booting instincts of his ancestors hang about him. Anyhow
> it is better than twelve rooms over a Post Office. I wonder
> Plunket did not offer you the second pair back over a gin-
> shop.

In a debate in the House on the rent charge for Dover House, Macdonald spoke strongly of the need to have somewhere of that calibre, in
keeping with the new appointment of Secretary for Scotland, and in
order to give the "greater dignity and effect to the interests of Scotland
in the country and in this House" intended by that appointment.

The new system had its problems from the start. The Home Office retained ultimate responsibility for law and order in Scotland, and
the division of powers between the Secretary for Scotland, the Lord

Advocate and the Home Secretary led inevitably to difficulties; there was also the fact that the Scottish Secretary did not have a seat in the Cabinet, nor (being a Peer) in the Commons. The new set-up, still to bed down, certainly did not help in dealing with the critical situation in the Highlands, especially at times when decisive action needed to be taken on the ground.

Moreover, the aristocratic attitude of the two chief figures to the new office of Secretary for Scotland was less than whole-hearted. Salisbury, in offering the position to the Duke of Richmond and Gordon, wrote:

> The work is not very heavy ... but measured by the expectations of the people of Scotland it is approaching Arch-angelic. We want a big man to float it – especially as there is so much sentiment about it. I think you seem pointed out by nature to be the man ... It really is a matter where the effulgence of two Dukedoms and the best salmon river in Scotland will go a long way.

To which the Duke replied:

> ... You know my opinion of the office, and that it is quite unnecessary, but the Country and Parliament think otherwise – and the office has been created, and someone must fill it. Under these circumstances I am quite ready to take it, and will do my best to make it a success (if this is possible!).

In thanking him Salisbury wrote:

> It makes a success at once – for the whole object of the move is to redress the wounded dignities of the Scotch people – or a section of them – who think that enough is not made of Scotland; & your taking the office will make the difference between the measure being a compliment to them, or a slight.

In his book *England 1870-1914* published in 1936, RGK Ensor described the period from June 1885 to July 1886 as "the most dramatic thirteen months in modern English party history". The Salisbury government was "in office but not in power" and did not survive the year 1885; it was defeated at the General Election in December and Gladstone formed his third cabinet at the beginning of February 1886. This administration in turn lasted only until August when Lord Salisbury formed his second cabinet and the Tories remained in power for the next six years.

Many of the most persistently urgent causes of the drama during the thirteen months referred to by Ensor were not English in origin but Irish and Scottish, with the strong movement for both Irish and Scottish home rule. The 1880s in the Highlands and Islands of Scotland were a troubled time.

The position of the crofters, lacking fixed legal rights, had become increasingly less secure, and that of the cottars (farm labourers who were without even the possession of any land) was worse. The old paternalistic clan system, under which for centuries an underlying sense of kinsmanship pertained, had broken down since the 1745 rising. The Highland Clearances had shown how harshly, how inhumanely, landlords (more and more commercially minded and often absentees), could treat their "kin". The old, rock-strong belief of the labourer that he had an inalienable, indeed Biblical, right to the land which he and his ancestors had occupied for generations still remained. The people did not own the land, nor were they able to own it; rather it could be said, as was said of the Aborigines in Australia, that the land owned them. It is no wonder that the crofters should wish to re-assert what they regarded as their birthright, particularly when their precarious living was further threatened by external forces. The potato famine in the 1840s had been a crucial blow, and in 1882 there were drastically poor returns for their crops and the herring fishings, which they relied on to supplement their meagre earnings from their crofts. At such times the pressures of over-population, exacerbated by the sub-division of holdings into smaller units, were most severely felt and the crofters' and cottars' conditions came in many parts close to destitution.

Frustration led to agitation for change. Through the Highland Land League (formed in 1883 as the Highland Land Law Reform Association) and its local branches they were able to give expression to their discontent and their aspirations, both in word and in action. As James Hunter in *The Making of the Crofting Community* states, it was

"more than a political party. It was a social movement, and as such
its inspiration and organisation came from below, from the crofting
community itself". For the first time the community was organised
as a powerful force in the land. After the election in November 1885
(when Macdonald was first elected MP) it had a voice – in fact four
voices – in Parliament; following the extended enfranchisement, four
out of five of the Highland crofting constituencies, traditionally held
by landowners, were won by HLLRA members. The Association was
founded on the same lines as the Irish Land League which had played
a crucial role in the agitation for reform leading to the Irish Land Act
passed under the Gladstone government in 1881. The Scottish reformers were well aware – many at first hand through their fishing opera-
tions across the Irish Sea – of events in Ireland where, although there
was a different tradition of tenant farming, many of the land problems
were the same. The Irish Act of 1881 had brought in security of tenure
and fair rents, two fundamental rights not enjoyed by Scottish crofters. In addition to the demand for these rights in Scotland there was a
need to satisfy the most pressing concern of all: the provision of more
land. Throughout the disturbances in the 1880s this was the most crucial issue, and the chief cause of confrontation with the forces of law
and order.

There had been instances at the beginning of the decade of concert-
ed non-payment of rents in parts of Skye – in Kilmuir and Glendale
in the north and in Braes near Portree. These followed the Irish example of rent strikes. On the Kilmuir estate a reduction in rents had been
won; in Glendale, as in Braes, the fight was for the return to the community of common grazing land taken in the past from their forebears.
At Braes in 1882 the most serious incidents to date of law-breaking
had occurred. The Landlord, Lord Macdonald, brought summonses
of removal against a number of tenants for arrears of rent, and in
April a sheriff officer sent to serve the eviction orders was assaulted
by a mob of over 100 people, and the summonses were burned. In
thus preventing an official of the law from carrying out an order of
the court the crofters had committed the crime of deforcement. The
Lord Advocate of the day, JB Balfour (later Lord Kinross) ordered the
arrest of five of the ring leaders and for the first time Sheriff Ivory, the
Sheriff of Inverness-shire, entered centre-stage. At his request the local
police, inadequate in number (and perhaps not best-fitted to cope with

the situation), were reinforced by a contingent from the Glasgow Con-
stabulary, and the sheriff went to Braes with a force of fifty policemen
to arrest the five men. They succeeded, but an angry crowd of crofters
and their wives tried to prevent the force returning to Portree with the
arrested men. The police were stoned and assaulted with any weapon
that came to hand; they in turn made a series of baton charges and
eventually fought their way through to the Portree road with their
prisoners. There were injuries suffered on both sides in what came
to be known as "The Battle of the Braes", the repercussions of which
spread rapidly as news of the bitter confrontation became known locally and in the world outside. The crofters of Braes were not shaken
in their resolve; they still refused to pay rents or to remove their cattle
from Ben Lee, as they had been ordered. A decree of Suspension and
Interdict against them was obtained in the Court of Session in Edinburgh, but the Messenger at Arms was prevented by "a riotous mob"
(in Sheriff Ivory's words) from serving the court orders on many of
the crofters. This was in early September 1882; later that month Sheriff Ivory made his first request to the government for a military force
to be sent to assist the police. The Lord Advocate (JB Balfour), at that
time still the chief Scottish Minister, backed this, but the request was
turned down by the government. The Braes trouble continued – in
October a further contingent of a Messenger at Arms and police was
prevented from entering the township. Matters were resolved, at least
temporarily, at the end of the year, by Lord Macdonald agreeing to
lease Ben Lee to the crofters.

There were other trouble spots in Skye, most notably at Glendale
where a more organised defiance of the landlords and the law prevailed, led by John Macpherson and the other "Glendale martyrs".
The authorities could not turn a blind eye to the state of lawlessness
there; there were not only wholesale rent strikes, but land was tak-
en by crofters for their own use; the police and court officers were
physically stopped from going into certain parts and prevented from
enforcing the law. Eventually, in January 1883, the Cabinet was persuaded by JB Balfour that troops should be sent to assist the police in
the arrest of the five Glendale leaders. However, before they were despatched Malcolm McNeill, a man conversant with conditions in the
Highlands and Islands as administrator of the Poor Law there, and a
Gaelic speaker, was sent on the first of his government missions: to try

to obtain the agreement of the crofters to the five leaders submitting to trial. This they did; the five were tried in Edinburgh and each sentenced to two months' imprisonment. Undeterred, the Glendale crofters persisted in their rent strike and the sheriff officer sent to serve summonses of removal against forty-five of them was prevented by a large crowd from doing so.

The agitation spread also to other islands – Tiree, Barra and Lewis – and to the North West Highlands. It was clear that the grievances were deep-seated and not capable of resolution without some fundamental reforms of the system. In face of the declining situation the government in February 1883 appointed a Royal Commission, with Lord Napier as chairman and McNeill as secretary, "to inquire into the condition of the Crofters and Cottars in the Highlands and Islands of Scotland". The setting up of the HLLRA at the same time ensured that the momentum of agitation was maintained. The Napier Commission gathered evidence at first hand up and down the land, starting appropriately at Braes. Crofters were able to speak openly, without fear or favour of their own hardships, revealing a long history of deprivation and insecurity. When it came out in 1884 the Commission's report exposed the worst aspects of the crofting system, but fell short of satisfying all the individual demands of the crofters, or cottars, while the landlords felt its recommendations to be a dangerous incursion into their rights of ownership. Having regard to the problem of over-congestion and the increasing practice, with the steady growth of population, of sub-dividing into smaller and even less economical units, the report recommended security of tenure for crofts only of over six acres and gave no protection to the cottars. It also proposed that the traditional townships should be re-formed as local communes, and where there was not sufficient land for their purposes they should have certain rights of purchase over adjoining land in private ownership. The report did not bring peace – quite the reverse when the limitations of its proposals became clear. The HLLRA at its first Annual Conference in September 1884 approved a manifesto – "the Dingwall Programme" – setting out the basic necessities for reform, including provision, on the lines of the Irish Land Act, for security of tenure, a system of fair rents and compensation for improvements carried out on their crofts by crofters. It also advocated a redistribution of land to enlarge crofting townships and to form new ones. There were no immediate signs of Gladstone's government taking steps to implement even the Napier recommendations, and further serious disturbances soon occurred in various parts. The bitterness against the landowners and their managers, and against the police who were widely regarded as agents for the landlords (crofters holding more respect for the army through loyalty to the Crown and their strong tradition of military service), spilled over into acts of violence and intimidation of a kind which added a new dimension to the non-payment of rents: seizure of land, destruction of dykes and fences, and other tactics. "The defiant spirit of lawlessness" which Lord Lovat, the Lord Lieutenant of Inverness, had the year before referred to as spreading over the Isle of Skye, was all too evident.

Reports from the chief constable and the Lord Advocate to the Home Office at this time graphically show the serious state of affairs in South Uist. One report in August 1884 from the chief constable annexed a "seditious circular" which read:

Highlandmen!

Crofters, cottars, dellars and all others! Stand up like men before your oppressors. Demand restoration of the rights of which you have been robbed. Do not rest satisfied until you have obtained them. If they are refused you then act for yourselves.

Rules for guidance in the struggle for freedom from landlord tyranny:

Spare human life. Kill no man except it be in self-defence. Destroy the enemy's property. The enemy is the landlord, the agents, the capitalist, and the Parliament which makes and maintains inhuman and iniquitous laws. Cut down the telegraph wires and posts. Carry away the wires. Destroy the instruments. Stop the mail-carts. Destroy the letters etc. Roll rocks and boulders on to the railway line. Tear up the rails, and do all other damage possible. Burn the property of all obnoxious landlords, agents etc. Set fire to the heather. Destroy the game. Disturb the deer. Poison the dogs.

The toilers of England and the millions of disinherited are watching your actions. Their hearts are with you in your battle for right and liberty.

God save the people!

And the Lord Advocate in one report wrote "During Saturday night the church at which Lady Cathcart was expected to attend on the following day was entered by a window, and the pulpit, Bible etc as well as some seats, were smeared with petroleum".

Both he and the chief constable advised that the use of a military or naval force might well be necessary to maintain order, and that the police force might need to be armed with revolvers.

In parts of Skye – in particular Kilmuir – guerrilla-type activities resulted in "no-go areas" where the police and court officials were unable and often unwilling to go. The authorities could not be expected to allow this explosive situation to continue. In the autumn of 1884, following a request from the chief constable of Inverness-shire, the government agreed that the Skye police force should be issued with arms, and fifty revolvers and 1000 rounds of ammunition were sent. It was realised that they would also require military protection and in November a force of 300 marines was sent to Skye on a troopship, supported by a gun-boat and a MacBrayne steamer, "Lochiel". Strict provisions as to the use of the military force were laid down. In such a sensitive area, and with such a headstrong and autocratic sheriff as Ivory, who regularly led the enforcers of law and order on the ground, it was essential to have the lines of conduct clearly demarcated, the role of the marines being distinguished and, so far as possible, kept apart from that of the police, so that there should be no suggestion of anything approaching martial law. It was an uneasy situation. The sheriff officers were still exposed in trying to serve the writs and court orders; the Liberal government, through the Home Secretary Sir William Harcourt, would not allow any military protection for this purpose. Deforcements continued, and although the marines were able to assist the police with a show of force on occasions where arrests were to be made, the overall effect of the military presence was very limited. During the normal summer lull when the crofting men were away at the fishing, the marines and extra police were withdrawn from Skye (in June 1885) but the Lord Advocate (Balfour) warned the Admiralty at the time that a government force might well be required in Lewis.

Gladstone introduced a Crofters Bill, incorporating some of the Napier recommendations but based more on the Irish Land Act of 1881. This fell when Gladstone resigned in June. Lord Salisbury took over and formed his first cabinet. Even though a new era in the conduct of Scottish affairs had begun with the re-instatement of the Scottish Office, the government was a minority one, unable to wield power, and there was little noticeable change in administration during its brief term

In Parliament, the dominant Scottish issue continued to be the Highland troubles. Disturbances continued in Skye and elsewhere. By mid-September Sheriff Ivory was pressing the Scottish Office for military aid, "disclaiming all responsibility for the consequences" if it was not granted. Regularly, sometimes several times in a week, police and other reports were transmitted to him by the Secretary for Scotland, with copies being sent to the Lord Advocate and, after he had dealt with them, sent on to the Home Office. These reports show clearly the nature and severity of the problem the Scottish Secretary and Macdonald were faced with in trying to maintain and restore law and order. Writing to the Duke of Richmond and Gordon in September 1885, Macdonald (as Lord Advocate) states: "The population is at present in a ferment against their local superiors". Non-payment of rents and rates was common; the collector of rates at Portree wrote of his inability to get a sheriff officer to serve summonses for rates, and one sheriff officer explained, in declining to serve summonses, that he did not wish "to have a hand in shortening his days voluntarily". The Valtos (Skye) crofters were reported as "determined to oppose Sheriff Officers even though all the police in Scotland are there to protect them". Where they were unable to collect rents the landlords too withheld payment of rates, resulting in a lack of funds for certain Parochial Boards such as Strath in Skye, and threatening the closure of schools and poor-houses. Sheriff Ivory persistently requested a government force be sent, but Macdonald advised against such action; he prepared a minute in October and communicated with the Secretary of State at the Home Office (Sir Richard Cross) on the subject. The landowners in the Western

Isles sent a Memorial to the Secretary for Scotland urging that immediate measures be taken "to vindicate the law". Their fear was that if
no action was taken no rents whatever would be paid at the approaching term of Martinmas. For their part the people hoped (but maybe
largely did not expect) that changes in the land laws would be made.
This aspect of reform did have the serious attention of the government
who intended to introduce "a comprehensive measure". Macdonald
himself was "busy in preparing to meet the crofter difficulties to the
best of his power", as he later informed the House of Commons in the
debate of the first reading of the Crofters (Scotland) (No 2) Bill in February 1886. As he said, he was specially interested "as being myself a
Highlander and the son of a Highlander" and he trusted that "we shall
be able to bring to an end this difficult and distressing subject which at
present is disturbing so many minds".

Macdonald's attitude to the use of the military in the enforcement
of the law was spelled out in his letter to Sheriff Ivory of 9th January
1886:

> What are the cases that have occurred in which a reasonably
> sufficient force of police have been so resisted in doing their
> duty, that a magistrate, if he had had a military force availa-
> ble, would have been justified in using it to aid the police, be-
> cause the latter, using their own force firmly and unflinching-
> ly, were overcome by violence? … I hold distinctly that even
> where a military force is present, in readiness to assist the po-
> lice, it cannot be used, till first a reasonably sufficient force
> of police for the contemplated emergency has made a deter-
> mined and courageous effort and been overcome. Under no
> circumstances could soldiers be employed to act instead of,
> or as additional, police. They could only be employed to act
> when there was demonstration that the police were overcome
> by superior force, after all reasonable effort.

Macdonald took his seat in the Commons in January 1886. With
the Duke of Richmond and Gordon in the Lords he acted as chief
spokesman in the Commons for his party on Scottish affairs; as Lord
Advocate, before Gladstone's government took over for a brief spell,
he made his first major speech in the House during the Answer to the

Queen's Speech. The subject was the severe agricultural depression of the times, which was to be a constantly recurring theme especially in relation to the situation in the Highlands and Islands. He gave a remarkably assured performance, clearly taking to the setting of the House like an inveterate actor to the stage. (He was aptly dubbed "the drama-loving Lord Advocate"). The style as much as the content of his speech display many of the characteristics of the man. He set the problem in the context of the general prevailing depression; there could never be:

> a long and severe depression in a country like ours without that depression spreading its wave of misery beyond those who cultivated the soil … these things could not be considered in a narrow spirit, or in reference to a state of depression applicable to one industry alone. Agricultural depression reacted, and must always do so, upon the welfare of the whole community.

The problem could not be solved "by any empirical or carelessly thought out remedies", it was necessary to look at the long term and at practical solutions. One suggestion he favoured was that capital should be found "to enable tenants to carry on their farms and work them better than they could do at the present time, in consequence of their having lost so much and being so depressed in mind". He introduced a lighter note by having a dig at Gladstone (who was something of a *bête noire* to him) for a suggestion he had once made that farmers should take to growing strawberries. As became a custom with him, he treated the House to a personal reminiscence which had some peripheral bearing on the matter under debate: in this case his knowledge of the "hinds" (farm workers) of Berwickshire, "one of the best farmed counties in the world", where he spent the summer months of his youth. He knew no "more comfortable set of people for their position in life". "What was wanted in the case of labourers was continuous and reasonably paid work" but they could never have that if they had "an overgrown population". This led him on to the ever emotive topic of emigration, on which he spoke plainly. Over-population, he said, "must lead either to emigration into the towns where the workmen would compete one against the other or to some land where there was less competition". He said they would never be rid of the difficulties with the labouring population of Britain as long as MPs pretended there was no benefit in labourers going abroad. They could not possibly sustain surplus population when wages were low; they could not raise wages until they had enough work and just the proper number of people to do it. They might fight as they pleased against that law; but that law would defeat them in the end. As regards emigration, all in that house belonged to the "better classes" in life, and they supported emigration. There was scarcely a man with a large family who had not one son either in India, Australia or America; when men went about to persuade the population that it was cruelty to induce them to emigrate, they did a grievous harm to the ignorant people whom they deceived. He concluded by explaining that he had not alluded to the Crofter question as there would be another opportunity later.

This speech shows many of the mixed facets of the man – the strengths and the limitations. The logic of the conclusions are worked out from practical considerations. He was innovative, but he was not a philosophical abstract thinker, with the result that, although he did look at the human side of a question, a sense of perceptive human feeling could be lacking. His Parliamentary speeches contain a mixture of the weighty and the light; humour is often used, not always appropriately. The note to the Spy cartoon of him in *Vanity Fair*[1] refers to his ability to raise a laugh even on so serious an issue as the crofting problem. While he clearly commanded the attention of the House, he must have irritated opponents at times by appearing light-hearted, using humour in a deflective or simply imperceptive way. One Scots MP described his usual manner in debate as "gambolling gracefully like a whale in a field of clover".

Agitation for reform continued strongly in the Highlands and Islands. It was clear that action had to be taken. In fact the one major piece of legislation passed during the 1886 Gladstone government's brief period in office was the Crofters Act. The revived Bill gave effect to the main proposals of the HLLRA, introducing fixity of tenure for crofters, compensation for improvements made by them, and a system for the fixing of fair rents through a new body, the Crofters

[1] (See Illustrations)

Commission. However, it was based on the Irish Land Reforms and did not meet all of the main recommendations of the Napier Commission, chiefly in regard to the need for more land for crofters, who in the words of its report in 1884 "suffered from undue contraction of the area of holdings". The Bill provided for only very limited enlargement of crofts. From the outset it met with much opposition.

In the House of Commons, Macdonald made a key speech on the Bill. It was in character that at the start he expressed the hope that "Hon Members would forgive him if they found what he had to say, and the mode in which he said it, rather dry and rather unlike what he hoped his usual style of addressing them was". He criticised the Bill as not effectively dealing with the situation: "It was a Bill that could have no other result than to produce (if it did produce, which he greatly doubted) a temporary alleviation of the difficulties of the present situation, but which would not in the near future bring about any results which should meet these difficulties". This was because it ignored the Napier Commission report and "the distinct and clear facts which had been ascertained since that Royal Commission sat". In his view this was due to money; the recommendations which would be a burden on the Exchequer had been cast aside. He looked at the various provisions from the landlords' as well as the tenants' viewpoint, spelling out the practical consequences, economic and otherwise. On rents, for example, he said that if it were found that they were too high the result would be "that it would become more certain than ever that the population could not be supported from the profits of the produce of the soil alone"; he stated that on present figures the total productive power of the soil for each person in the Highlands and Islands amounted to not more than £3.12s or £3.15s a year, which was less than the amount paid for the support of paupers. The practice of "destructive sub-division necessarily aggravated every evil in these places". If they sub-divided down to the size of the small croft, it would be impossible for the family to obtain subsistence.

He doubted very much whether the proposals to give increased land to crofters would work. The land was not to be held and cultivated by individual crofters; certain hill land suitable for pasture was to be given to a township or group of crofters to hold in common. But the Bill made no provision to ensure that those who took the land would be able to stock it so that they could make a beneficial use of it, and the landlord could receive a reasonable return. Unless capital was made available for the working of this additional land the experiment must fail.

He referred to "the real difficulties of the case", which he specified as the population and its natural increase; the deficiency of outflow for energy towards acquirement of means other than by agriculture; the defective nature of communication; and the difficulty of education.

The increase in population of the Islands in the last century had resulted in reducing the average acreage per head to nineteen acres, whereas no less than fifty-seven acres was regarded as sufficient to support an individual. This showed, he said, the necessity for other industry than agriculture, but the Bill was completely silent on this. It also did not include the recommendation of the Commission that the measures proposed for increasing the holding of land should not apply to those holding very small plots of land which the Commissioners fixed at £6 per annum. Nor was any notice taken of the cottar question. As the Commissioners had reported, it was essential that the people on these smallholdings be withdrawn. "The land had been sub-divided so that it was impossible in many cases for the holdings to be enlarged. How were the people to be withdrawn?" There were only two ways of doing it. One was that industry should be developed upon the spot. The other was that industry should be found for them elsewhere to which they could be removed. The only industry in the Highlands was fishing, which he said "was capable of vast extension for the benefit of the population of the Western Highlands", but absolutely no notice of it was taken in the Bill.

The Bill, he went on, was also silent on another matter – most unpalatable to many – which the Napier Commission had declared to be unavoidable: emigration.

> Why had that recommendation not been given effect to? Emigration was unavoidable in the case of many others than the crofters. It was impossible to find employment for everyone in this country and many of our sons had to go to all parts of the world in search of situations. The feeling against emigration was really a sentimental one, and would be removed if those people only knew the altered conditions now as compared with what existed thirty or forty years ago. The means of communication were much easier and education enabled

relatives at a distance to be in constant communication, so that the abhorrence to separation need not be what it was in former times. The Commissioners said emigration, properly conducted, was an indispensable remedy, and unavoidable.

He instanced what he claimed was the success of the emigration scheme set up by Lady Gordon Cathcart in South Uist.

On education, he sincerely trusted that the teaching of Gaelic should not be stamped out. That would be "a monstrous cruelty, particularly as the use of Gaelic was the only way by which religious intercourse could be kept up between the older and the younger members of a family, that they should both be able to use the same Bible" and at the same time the teaching of English should be promoted to "enable the people to converse and to carry on their work in other places. Popular education ... would lay open the whole world, with all its resources, to the most secluded inhabitants of the glens." Utopian schemes were of no use. The poor they would always have. Neither would anything which only encouraged mere sentiment do the slightest good. The best spirit in which they could proceed was to help the poor in a double way, by giving them every assistance that would not destroy their industry and self-reliance, and by devoting attention to every means of improving the lot of those who might remain in the Highlands and Islands. He hoped they would be able "to cultivate a spirit of manly pluck and energy like other people".

The Secretary for Scotland in Gladstone's government (Trevelyan) refuted Macdonald's statement that the government hung up all the recommendations which would involve expenditure of public money and took only the others which would cost nothing. They took the Commissioners' cardinal recommendation relating to the giving of grazing land to crofters (this provoked shouts of "No, no!" and cries of "arable land"). When Trevelyan referred to the cottars Macdonald interjected to say he had misunderstood what he said, which was that the Bill would not enable the cottar and small crofter to attain any better position in life than he has at present. "I say so still", he added.

Trevelyan put the arguments against including emigration in the Bill saying it is a Crofters Bill and applies crofter remedies to crofter circumstances. "A very special Bill, referring to a very special population living in a very special district under very special evils". But congestion and want of work are not special evils confined to a special population. He hoped advantages of emigration would reach the West Highlands but he was still against including a public machinery of emigration when agrarian agitation was going on. Macdonald considered the emigration question to be inseparable from the overall problem; it came down to a question of money.

The Crofters Act was passed but the Gladstone government floundered on the Irish Home Rule Bill (very much Gladstone's brainchild), which was defeated after intense debate, through the opposition of dissentients within the Liberal party led by Joseph Chamberlain and supported by the Conservatives. Gladstone went to the country, which showed even less support for home rule, and he was heavily defeated. Salisbury returned to office with a sizeable majority.

Chapter 8

The Troubles Continue

A J Balfour (Salisbury's nephew) became Secretary for Scotland, although at first without a seat in Cabinet. Macdonald was reappointed Lord Advocate. William Blackwood wrote to his friend on 3rd August 1886:

> *My Dear Jack,*
>
> Delighted to see you are to be our Lord Advocate again although if you had desired it I have no doubt Lord Salisbury would have given you "The Secretary of State for Scotland" appointment for which in my opinion you are also very eminently well qualified. It would I am sure have been a very popular appointment and more so a great deal than Balfour's who whatever he may be in England is not I think well known in "dear old Scotland" which you are.

Blanche Dugdale in her biography of Balfour quotes a letter dated July 30th 1886 from Lord Cranbourne (Salisbury's son) to Balfour in which he says: "The reasons you are to be Secretary (for Scotland) are sufficiently obvious e.g. you were chosen to lead the party in the Crofters Debate instead of Macdonald to whom it would naturally have fallen and most wisely so chosen". The disturbances in the Highlands and Islands in particular had shown up the highly unsatisfactory division of powers between the Home Secretary, Lord Advocate and Secretary for Scotland. Under the Secretary for Scotland Act 1885 the Lord Advocate remained answerable to the Home Secretary and not to the Secretary for Scotland. This had already led to muddled and ineffectual decision-making when co-ordinated, firm action was urgently required.

Within two weeks of his appointment Balfour set about obtaining greater powers for his office. He and Macdonald prepared Memoranda on the subject for the Cabinet. Balfour drew attention to "the extreme inconvenience, and even danger, of leaving things precisely as they are", and suggested that by "mutual arrangement between the Home Office and the Scotch (*sic*) Office the practical executive supremacy, in so far as it is possessed by the former, may be transferred to the latter, as a temporary expedient, without the intervention of an Act of Parliament". The Scottish Secretary, he said, was generally regarded inside and outside Parliament as the person responsible for dealing with the disorders in the west of Scotland:

> But, as the Office is at present constituted by statute, the Secretary for Scotland has no more to do with restoring law and order in Skye and in Tyree than he has in restoring order in Belfast and in Kerry. The whole duty lies with the Home Secretary and with the Lord Advocate, who are not required to consent, or even to keep informed, the Secretary at Dover House.

The difficulties would be enormously increased, he maintained, if the authority for dealing with the situation were unnecessarily divided, instead of having a strong central authority (as in Ireland) "with direct control of a practically unlimited force of police, and having at its command constant and accurate information with respect to all parts of the country".

Balfour specified two main powers which the Scottish Secretary would require to have: the first was that of controlling the sending of troops to aid a local authority – "in reality the sole lever which enables any Minister to influence the policies of the local authorities"; and the second related to the Lord Advocate. Balfour proposed that where, under the existing system, the Lord Advocate "informs the Home Secretary of his proceedings in purely legal matters or requires his advice and direction on questions of policy, he should in future inform or consult instead the Secretary for Scotland".

Macdonald took the legalistic view that nothing could be done without an Act of Parliament. "If the Secretary for Scotland were to

exercise powers which are not conferred on him by the Statute under which his office came into existence his action would be irregular
and I should think invalid. Delegation by an Officer of State of duties
imposed on him by Statute or ancient custom is plainly illegal". As
regards the position of the Lord Advocate he pointed out that the Act
setting up the office of Secretary for Scotland declared that nothing in
the Act "shall prejudice or interfere with any rights, powers, privileges or duties vested in or imposed on the Lord Advocate by virtue of
any Act of Parliament or custom". If the control of law and order was
transferred to the Secretary for Scotland the Lord Advocate would be
subordinate to the Secretary for Scotland. "He would, although himself an officer of State, holding an ancient and important office, be
responsible to an official who is not a Secretary of State. To this no
Lord Advocate could submit on any private arrangement between two
other officials".

Balfour brushed aside Macdonald's arguments referring to "the
miseries of etiquette". He wrote to Lord Salisbury:

> The present Lord Advocate is an excellent fellow and a per-
> sonal friend. But *no* Lord Advocate likes being subordinated
> to a Minister *not* in the Cabinet; the tradition of the Office, ac-
> cording to which the principal Secretary of State was the only
> official superior to the Scotch Law Officers, is too strong at the
> Edinburgh Bar.

Before the end of 1886 Balfour did have a seat in the Cabinet, but he
was soon moved on, being appointed Secretary for Ireland. It was
under his successor as Secretary for Scotland, Lord Lothian, that the
amending legislation went through.

Balfour won the day and responsibility for law and order was transferred from the Home Office to the Scottish Office, the Lord Advocate
being responsible in future to the Secretary for Scotland. The informal
arrangement left many uncertain areas in the relationship between the
Lord Advocate and the Secretary for Scotland. Even after the passing
of the Secretary for Scotland Amendment Act in 1887 Lord Lothian
felt there was a need for a better definition of the relative positions
and duties of the two offices. As HJ Hanham wrote in an article on
The Creation of the Scottish Office 1881-87: "The Secretary for Scotland

continued to regard himself as in a sense a competitor with the Lord Advocate for control over the legal system and the Prime Minister acted as arbiter between them". Gradually the Lord Advocate gave up more of the political reins. Within a generation after the passage of the Secretary for Scotland Act the Lord Advocate had ceased to be thought of as primarily a political figure and had come to be regarded as little more than the government's principal legal adviser in Scotland.

The new regime did not have to wait before exerting its authority. Trouble had arisen in July 1886 on the Island of Tiree where crofters had prevented the new tenant of a farm (owned by the Duke of Argyll) from taking possession of it. The Duke obtained interdicts in the Court of Session in Edinburgh against fifty-one crofters to prevent them taking illegal possession of the farm. Notices of the Interdict had to be served on the men by the sheriff officer and, anticipating difficulty he was escorted by twenty-one policemen and sixteen commissionaires. This force proved neither large or strong enough to effect the service; a crowd shouting and brandishing sticks prevented the sheriff officer from serving the notices, surrounding him "in a masterful manner" in the words of the court indictment. They had also threatened to destroy the two gigs which accompanied the party and throw them over the cliff. The Liberal Secretary for Scotland at the time authorised the sending of a military expedition to Tiree, but within a matter of days Balfour had taken over, and on his second day in office, a large force consisting of fifty policemen with 250 marines and 120 bluejackets landed on the island. On 3rd August the Sheriff of Argyll sent a telegram to the Lord Advocate Macdonald at Dover House stating that "if arrests are to be made it would be well that instructions be sent as early as possible while the marines and constables are here". The next day Balfour telegraphed to Macdonald: "As a matter of public policy it seems most important arrests of persons who deforced police should be effected with least possible delay. If you agree will you give necessary instructions, as it seems to me the only doubt is whether arrests should be made for deforcement or mobbing". On 6th August Macdonald sent a telegram to the sheriff: "The Lord Advocate considers it most important that you at once determine what persons should be arrested – proceed to have them arrested and questioned without a moment's delay". Six men were arrested the next day and subsequently eight in all stood trial in Edinburgh in October.

Macdonald as Lord Advocate led the Crown prosecution. There was evidence that if the force had continued with its attempt to serve the Notices of Interdict bloodshed would have resulted, and a threat was made to the sheriff officer that if he went on he would not come back alive. The drivers were also told they would be "done for". However, no one was hurt throughout the disturbance. The jury found all the men guilty but "strongly recommended them to the leniency of the Court". Five were given six months' imprisonment, and the other three, four months. These sentences, clearly aimed to deter others, were severely criticised in many quarters as over-severe. They bore no relation to previous sentences for such charges, and it was pointed out that in the City of Glasgow Bank case where huge sums were involved, some of the accused received sentences of only eight months imprisonment.

Malcolm McNeill was sent on a confidential mission of inquiry into the condition of the Western Highlands and Islands. John Macdonald was to have undertaken this; he wanted to go, but it was rightly considered that he would be too conspicuous, and it did not accord with his public position. McNeill was much more suitable for the task having been Secretary to the Napier Commission and a Gaelic speaker. He reported to Balfour in October, and subsequently gave a further memo on possible state-aided schemes of emigration.

After Tiree, Skye became the main trouble spot. Balfour and Macdonald were much concerned about the enforcement of the law for the collection of rents and rates which had been widely withheld in some areas, notably Glendale and Kilmuir. In his Memo to the Cabinet of 15th September, Balfour set out proposals for dealing with the situation. He referred to the "uselessness of the police"' who the locals "held in the uttermost contempt", regarding them as emissaries of the landlord, a view fortified by the fact that under Scots Law the local police rate was levied entirely on owners of land. He had consulted with the Lord Advocate and other law officers and the remedies proposed were to increase and arm the police, which would be likely to lead to bloodshed, and to support police with marines, for example in serving writs for rents. Action to distrain (in Scots, *poind*) goods for rent and rates alike should be taken against defaulting landlords as well as tenants. The law officers agreed with the policy proposed. "Its execution depends on the discretion of the chief executive authority on the spot, who is entirely independent of any central control and whose management in the past has certainly not been above criticism".

Sheriff Ivory was pressing for a military force to be despatched of which he could take virtual command on the ground. A detachment of marines was sent to Skye in October, but Balfour told Ivory that it could not be used until landowners were served with writs for rates arrears in the same way as crofters for rent arrears. This had not been done. Landowners had been withholding rates on the basis that they had not received the portion of rates due with the rents from their tenants.

The marines were especially required in support of attempts to carry out orders for poinding the goods of crofters who had not paid their rates, where organised resistance was expected. The process of poinding was (as it still is) detested as the most inhumane form of legal action against a debtor. A detachment of twenty marines and twelve policemen under a superintendent accompanied the sheriff officers and the local sheriff-substitute and sheriff clerk depute to one likely trouble spot in Kilmuir on 25th October. This was the township of Bornaskitaig. When the party approached a horn was blown and the inhabitants immediately began to assemble. At one house where a writ was to be served a crowd of about 100 had gathered, a line of more than twenty women with their arms linked together blocked the door, supported by their menfolk on either side who prevented the police from moving the women away. The sheriff-substitute ordered the police to move the women away from the doorway with as little violence as possible. The women kicked and hit out at the constables; after the arrest of two men who had prevented the police getting through, the crowd pelted the police and the sheriff with clods of earth and "filth of all kinds from a manure heap". The marines, with bayonets drawn, held back the crowd, more arrests were made and eventually the sheriff officer was able to carry out "a keyhole service". Six men stood trial before a jury at the High Court in Edinburgh in December accused of mobbing, rioting and assault on a sheriff and officers of the law in the execution of their duty. Addressing the jury Macdonald, who led the prosecution, spelled out the "very lamentable" consequences of resistance to civil process: "in the free exercise of civil process in this country rests all our liberties". A man was not entitled to take the law into his own hands and "no one should take upon himself to resist the operation of that law when it is put in force against him". There was no doubt, he said, about the mobbing and rioting. "If people remain in a crowd which is acting unlawfully, and do not protest against its action, even though they personally do nothing, they become participants in the action. That is the law". The judge (Lord Mure) in his charge to the jury confirmed the mobbing and rioting, and the assault by at least one of the accused on the sheriff could hardly be in doubt. The jury unanimously found all guilty of mobbing and rioting, two not guilty of assault, and the charge of assault against four others not proven. They recommended the utmost leniency. Sentences of three months' imprisonment were pronounced.

Macdonald also led the prosecution in the High Court in two other Skye cases involving the deforcement of the sheriff officer, Alexander Macdonald. One incident occurred at Herbusta on the same day as the Bornaskitaig trouble, and the other the following day at Garalapin near Portree. The indictments in each case laid it on with a heavy trowel and were severely criticised by the presiding judge, Lord Young. The Garalapin one stated that:

> A mob of riotous and evil-disposed persons … did wickedly and feloniously assemble in a riotous and tumultuous manner and in breach of public peace and to the alarm of the lieges, for the unlawful purposes of over-awing, intimidating and obstructing the said Alexander Macdonald by threats, force and violence and preventing, or endeavouring to prevent, him from fulfilling his duty of executing or serving the said charges of payment … and the said mob … did, then and there, conduct themselves in a violent, riotous and tumultuous manner … and did in a masterful manner surround and use violent and threatening language towards the said Alexander Macdonald (and his assistants) … and the said mob did behave otherwise in a turbulent and violent manner

Lord Young at the start of the hearing told the jury that the charge was set forth at unnecessary length. The question was whether the prisoners or any of them formed part of a mob and prevented the sheriff officer from discharging his duty. In the Herbusta case he said he had to point out there was in the indictment a great deal of superfluous and unduly inflated and exaggerated language, and he would like to suggest to the learned Counsel – who although they did not draw up the indictments, revised them – that such "had better be struck out". Putting such "superfluity of technicality" before a jury was, he thought, peculiar to Scotland. It did not happen south of the Tweed because it was thought misleading, but custom had arisen here and it was difficult to move away from it. This was changed by the Criminal Procedure (Scotland) Act 1887 introduced by Macdonald in the Commons.

The evidence in the Garalapin case did establish that at least some of the eight accused were among a crowd of about thirty who confronted the sheriff officer's party. They prevented the officer from going to the houses with the charges, threatening that if he tried he would have his head and his boxes broken. Sticks and graips were brandished, but no actual violence was used. There was particularly strong animosity against Sheriff Officer Alexander Macdonald, on account of his involvement in two notorious incidents: the burning down of a crofter's house after evicting him and his family, and the poinding of a baby in the house of a crofter. Counsel for two of the accused in this case and in the Herbusta one sought to question Alexander Macdonald about these - and another occasion where he was said to have executed a warrant of poinding in the house of a crofter while his wife was in the pains of labour - in order to show that he entertained malice against the crofters which affected his credibility. Further, if it could be proved that this officer habitually treated the crofters in a cruel and tyrannical manner, this went to show that they were not resisting the law, but were resisting a lawless aggressor, who under cover of the law did what was unlawful. Lord Young, however, in both cases disallowed these questions. Whether the references to the sheriff officer's past misdemeanours affected the jury, it is, of course, impossible to say, but in the Garalapin case they found two of the accused (against whom the charges were withdrawn at the end of the proof stage) not guilty, and by a majority the others also not guilty.

At Herbusta the same sheriff officer was again prevented by a threatening crowd from carrying out his duty. Seven crofters stood trial before Lord Young and the same jury as in the Garalapin trial. The jury unanimously found the accused guilty but earnestly recommended four of them to the utmost leniency of the court. Lord Young sentenced the latter to one month imprisonment and the other three to two months.

Overcrowding and the lack of land – and the failure of the Crofters Act to meet this – remained the main problem, as well as the payment of rent. The petition sent to John Macdonald in September 1886 by crofters and others in Benbecula, South Uist, shows graphically the extremities of destitution and resignation which they and others like them had reached. The twenty-eight petitioners state they "are willing and desirous to leave our native homes and emigrate to the North West Territories of North America or to New Zealand". They have found it "utterly impossible to eke out livelihoods in our native island for the last number of years" and list five causes:

- Natural barrenness of the soil owing from having no mineral matter.
- Prices on stock have fallen so low and are still falling.
- Kelp manufacture is gone, which was a help to some of the crofter population of the island
- No improvements of any description carried on for a considerable time past.
- The island is densely overpopulated and shall not maintain more than one third of the present population.

It ends with a plea for help in laying the matter before Parliament immediately so that they can be given assistance "which shall enable us to proceed directly to some British colony, where we shall be able to better our present miserable condition". Lady Gordon Cathcart, the local landowner, who had a hand in assisting them in emigrating, must have helped in the drawing up of the petition. In forwarding it, she mentions that two of the signatories are in fact the chairman and secretary of the local Land League.

While Skye became more peaceful that winter; destitution – near desperation – led people elsewhere, on Lewis, to take ever more extreme action. The authorities were more stretched than ever to deal with it. Those authorities from the Secretary for Scotland down were severely criticised in Parliament and in the press for their handling of the situation in Skye. Sheriff Ivory's autocratic, repressive actions were particularly condemned. *The North British Daily Mail* (owned by Dr Charles Cameron, one of the Crofter MPs) vehemently campaigned against the sheriff, describing him as "an autocratic monarch of the Middle Ages" who thinks himself the King of Skye, "a firebrand whose removal is necessary for the peace of the Highlands". Among other actions it refers to the night raid headed by Sheriff Ivory with a police force, on the Herbusta crofters. It reports a deputation went to Balfour to put before him "the miseries of the Skye people", and to complain about the "Monomaniac" sheriff's conduct. They went away empty-handed, having found Balfour's air of, in the words of the newspaper, "the top boy in the class will now recite", more than usually pronounced.

At the end of the year a petition for Sheriff Ivory's removal, or failing that his suspension from office, was transmitted to the Scottish Office by Charles Fraser Mackintosh (another of the Crofter MPs who had himself been a member of the Napier Commission). Early in 1887, after physical threats against him, the sheriff was provided with bodyguards. The failure to grasp the profound ill-feeling provoked by Sheriff Ivory and to take proper action to curb him, did not help the authorities' cause in dealing with the troubles. Without him the necessary steps in carrying out the law could have been taken more readily in the humane manner which the chief constable wished. The sheriff had open disputes with the chief constable, particularly in relation to his trying to exercise control over the police, by-passing the chief constable of Inverness-shire.

John Macdonald did on a number of occasions have to rebuke Ivory on this and other matters. There were incidents involving the sheriff officer from Inverness, Alexander Macdonald, already mentioned for his part in the Garalapin case. In September 1886 he had evicted a tenant and his family in Strathglass, Inverness-shire, and proceeded to burn down the house and outbuildings. A parliamentary question was put to Balfour, and subsequently John Macdonald wrote to Ivory directing that "having acted in a most improper and perfectly unauthorised manner", he was to convey a severe reprimand to Sheriff Officer Macdonald at the instance of the Lord Advocate. Ivory prevaricated saying he awaited a report of another sheriff's (Blair) inquiry before taking any action.[1] A letter from the Crown Agent to Ivory repeated the instruction to administer a reprimand. Ivory replied that he had

---

[1] A pencilled note on Ivory's letter, reads: "This is characteristic. It surely ought to be enough for the Sheriff that the Lord Advocate has directed him to act in a particular way. Apparently he does not think so"

now read the report of Sheriff Blair and after careful perusal has arrived at the same conclusion as the Lord Advocate and accordingly has censured the sheriff officer and conveyed by desire of the Lord Advocate a severe reprimand. Nobody, it seems, was going to tell Ivory his business; he would do things in his own way, as and when it suited him. The reprimand had no effect, as a matter of days later the same sheriff officer was involved in an even more infamous incident. In valuing the contents of the house of a woman in Peiness, Skye, for a poinding sale, he included (along with a puppy dog at 1s) a cradle and child at 6d. Even Sheriff Ivory could not ignore or condone such heartless behaviour. He consulted with John Macdonald, sending him a draft letter to the sheriff officer referring to an inquiry carried out by Sheriff Hamilton who clearly established the charge of poinding the child, and which also mentioned that, although a charge "of personal violence" against the woman had not been established, there was "no doubt that you took hold of her and pushed her about in a manner that you had no right to do". The letter refers to Alexander Macdonald's "previous good record" in carrying out difficult duties which he was unwilling (and at first refused) to undertake. John Macdonald made alterations to the draft letter but did not in the end make the decision any heavier: surprisingly he adds that but for his past conduct he would have had Alexander Macdonald dismissed from the public service. "In consideration however of the high character which you have hitherto deservedly maintained I have with some hesitation arrived at the conclusion that I shall have sufficiently fulfilled my duty if I now severely censure you". It is quite remarkable that the incident of setting fire to the croft, dealt with earlier that same month by a reprimand, had been either overlooked – or more reprehensibly – not considered with due seriousness. All this, in its way, gives an insight into why the authorities provoked so much opposition in dealing with sensitive matters on the ground.

Relations between Ivory and the chief constable came to such a head that in December 1886 a formal complaint was made to the Secretary for Scotland and a memorial was submitted to John Macdonald and the other Scottish law officers for their opinion on various points of disagreement. Mainly these concerned the issuing of orders by Ivory that conflicted with – in some instances cut right across – the authority of the chief constable and the regulations under which he operated. On two or three occasions Ivory requested the inspector of

Mathew Norman Macdonald Hume WS
Sir John's father

Lt Gen Alexander Macdonald
by Sir John Watson Gordon

Lt Gen Sir John Macdonald GCB
by Sir John Watson Gordon

Norman Macdonald
of Bernisdale and
Scalpay, Skye
Sir John's grandfather

Adelaide Jeanette Doran
Sir John's wife

Agnes Hume
Sir John's stepmother

Sir John aged 9
by Robert T Ross

Sir John
by Sir Hubert von Herkomer

Man of Mark of Interrogation
Illustration in *Our Trip to Blumderland*
by Charles Doyle

Front cover
of *Our Trip to
Blumderland*,
designed by
Charles Doyle

Sir John
Captain of Royal &
Ancient Golf Club
9th Hole St. Andrews
by T Hodge

Sir John as Lord Advocate in House of Commons
Cartoon by Spy in Vanity Fair

Sir John: Lord Justice-Clerk
by Robert S Forrest

Sir John and S1

Sir John's
Funeral

police on Skye to make secret enquiries about the situation there, and to communicate directly with him, without reference to the chief constable. The inspector, in accordance with standing orders, informed the chief constable, who replied that all communications relating to police matters must be sent to him. This did not prevent the sheriff persisting in trying to deal privately with the inspector, for example to report to him "what is doing when the Lord Advocate is in Skye, what witnesses he examines, when and where", repeating the request when a Special Commissioner (McNeill) was sent instead. When the inspector asked to be allowed to report any enquiries, public or private, to the chief constable and to receive instructions through him, Sheriff Ivory declined. In August 1886 the sheriff issued an order that the standing police orders and instructions no longer had his approval. They were not to be acted on by the inspector, and the chief constable should issue an order to that effect. The chief constable pointed out that the orders could not be altered without agreement of the police committee, but Ivory insisted that he was entitled in the public interest to direct that any part no longer applied.

The memorial also referred to "open rupture" between Ivory and the chief constable on board HMS Humber in October 1886, during the expedition to Skye, with a force of marines. "The views of Sheriff Ivory and the Chief Constable regarding the rights and powers relating to the Government and discipline of the police force were diametrically opposed". Ivory altered the plan for the landing of the expeditionary force to serve writs, consulting only with the commander of the marines. The chief constable asked Ivory to give his order through him, but the sheriff repeated his order, and the chief constable replied that he refused to alter his arrangements. The expedition started under the charge of the sheriff-substitute and the chief constable. On his return the sheriff-substitute told the chief constable that if he found his position "uncomfortable and lowering in the eyes of the ship's Officers" he should return to Inverness. This he did.

The opinion of Macdonald, JPB Robertson (Solicitor General) and WM Rankine held that Sheriff Ivory had:

> gone beyond his legal powers as an Executive Officer of the Crown … (he) stands outside and forms no part of the organisation of the Police and has no power to control its disposition

and government as an organisation. The Sheriff's pretensions and proceedings regarding secret enquiries and instructions to subordinate officers were regarded as subversive of the discipline, which is the essential condition of such an organisation even in case of emergency.

The other main ground of complaint related to silver medals which Sheriff Ivory had specially made in July 1886 and presented to four constables bearing the insertion: "From Sheriff Ivory for zeal and activity, arrest of Parnell Valtos 13th January 1885". They were to be worn on watch chains. This contravened an official decision that extra awards would not be made, and it was also done without the chief constable's or any other police permission. The chairman of the police committee informed Sheriff Ivory of his opinion that the presentation and wearing of medals without government authority was inadmissible and "would intensify the dislike of Islanders for the Police and excite jealousy among members of the force". The opinion said there was nothing illegal in the presentation of medals as gifts, but the wearing of them on uniforms without permission of the police committee and the chief constable would be "plainly subversive of discipline", and if the sheriff intended they should be worn as a matter of duty, he acted *ultra vires*.[1]

The memorial itself ends with a note: "These (the facts set out) are the only cases of disagreement or ill feeling between the sheriff and the chief constable and the general accusation by the chief constable of discourtesy and overbearing conduct is otherwise unsupported and amply disproved". The government authorities seemed not to wish to know, or to be unable to make a sure assessment of the situation and act accordingly. Sheriff Ivory continued by and large on his merry way. There were soon further problems over "conflict of orders" issued by him; the police committee had to refer to the Secretary for Scotland for his decision over the sheriff communicating orders to the chief constable through a third party. Ivory said this was not the case – he

[1] Sheriff Ivory had also later, in December 1886, presented silver "ornaments" to some policemen for their part in making arrests at Garalapin "to be worn on watch chain as directed by your Lordship and if any one objects to my wearing same I will at once communicate to your Lordship", as acknowledgements from the police constable state. The Memorial to Crown Counsel must have been prepared before this was known about.

communicated in the usual way through the procurator fiscal as "his hand and agent". The matter was referred to John Macdonald as Lord Advocate, who commented that he could not for one moment accept that a procurator fiscal in Scotland is the sheriff's hand and agent in maintaining law and order, he is so as regards investigations into and detection of crime. It was improper for the procurator fiscal to interfere with the administration or working of the police in maintaining the peace. He could not as the representative of the sheriff give them any order connected with their duties, although he may use them to aid him in enquiries into alleged cases of crime. Sheriff Ivory, he said, should be told this distinctly. In fact, if he was not able to appreciate this rudimentary point he was surely not fit to be a sheriff.

The first adjudications on rent by the Crofters Commission in January 1887 helped to calm the situation. In addition to appreciable reduction of rent in many cases, the Commission declared the cancellation of arrears. Landowners, anticipating the loss of arrears often dating back some years, sought to obtain court orders for payment of these arrears before the Commission considered their rents. This led to the one confrontation in Skye that winter, when a sheriff officer attempting to serve summonses for payment of arrears at Elishader was physically prevented from doing so. Macdonald initially advocated that the crofters concerned should be arrested and brought to trial, but on consideration it was felt that this would lead to further trouble, considering the dubious morality of the landowners' tactics, and the fact that if pursued against a crofter it could lead to bankruptcy and consequently the loss of his house. In the event no action was taken, and the government introduced amending legislation to prevent such a move by landlords.

In the Commons one of the crofter MPs (Dr Cameron) called for a full inquiry into the administration of justice in Scotland. The complaints were directed against the conduct of Sheriff Ivory ("a judicial monster" as someone was reported to have called him), Sheriff Officer Macdonald, and the arrests and trials of the Tiree and Skye crofters. The Lord Advocate was attacked among other things for having these trials held in Edinburgh and not locally; in defending this Macdonald pointed out that if they had been tried before a sheriff and a jury there would have been a much greater outcry, because they would have been tried before Sheriff Ivory. He also made the point that cases of mobbing, rioting and deforcing officers of the law being so rare, they should be tried where the best legal talent can be found for their defence, and the best judicial officers to try them from the Bench. "Lord Young", he said, "in the last case tried, distinctly announced his opinion in open Court that the Lord Advocate of Scotland would have been guilty of a gross dereliction of duty if he had tried these cases in any other Court than the Supreme Court of the country".

Chapter 9

Clashmore, Park and Aignish

When AJ Balfour became Secretary for Ireland in March 1887, the Marquis of Lothian succeeded him as Secretary for Scotland. Balfour had subsumed without statutory authority the powers vested in the Home Secretary relating to law and order in Scotland – a necessary step in trying to establish more direct control over the Highland disturbances. Relations between the Scottish Office and the Home Office remained strained. Lothian's appointment meant a reversion to the previous situation of the Secretary for Scotland being in the Lords with the Lord Advocate in the Commons, and this added to the need for legislation to define the respective roles and powers of the Scottish Secretary, the Home Secretary, and the Lord Advocate. A Bill amending the Secretary for Scotland Act of 1885 was introduced in the Commons by Macdonald. Various Scottish MPs expressed dissatisfaction with the role of the Secretary for Scotland; the office had been created to increase efficiency in the administration of Scottish affairs, and to promote Scottish business in Parliament and for these purposes many (including Lord Lothian) felt he should have at least all the functions in Scotland which the Home Secretary had in England, and that he should have the rank of Secretary of State and thus a seat in the Cabinet (as had the Irish Secretary). There was a strong feeling that he should be a member of the House of Commons; with the Scottish Secretary in the House of Lords, Scottish members were worse off than before. The Lord Advocate was placed in a difficult position and was described as a sort of inferior under secretary, a kind of mouthpiece in the Commons, being the only official representing Scottish interests there. Now, with many administrative functions with which the Lord Advocate was not particularly qualified to deal, there was a

need to have the Scottish Secretary in the Commons. The Lord Advocate had his own duties to perform, and had also to act as the conduit
pipe through which the opinions of the Scottish Secretary were communicated to the Commons.

One member (Sir Geo Balfour) moved an amendment to add that
all the duties relating to the preparation of Bills, as well as those of the
Crown Agent, and of the Legal Secretary should be carried out under
the Secretary for Scotland, instead of the Lord Advocate, who had far
more important duties to perform, and would be far more dignified if
relieved of those responsibilities. This led Macdonald to interject that
the reference to the dignity of his office reminded him of the lines:

> It is all very well to dissemble your love,
> But why do you kick me downstairs?[1]

"It is proposed", he said, "to turn the Lord Advocate out of this House
and send him down to Scotland a mere legal officer … I prefer to remain a little longer. Although the Lord Advocate sometimes does
make mistakes regarding Bills, I think he is a very suitable officer to
attend to the drafting of Bills for Scotland". The amendment was withdrawn.

The 1887 Act was passed, transferring all the still remaining powers
of the Home Secretary to the Secretary for Scotland. There was no specific reference to the position of the Lord Advocate, which had been
left untouched by the previous Act, and the relationship between him
and the Secretary for Scotland remained ill-defined. In September 1888
Lord Lothian described it in a letter to Lord Salisbury as "very unsatisfactory and perplexing". By that time the government had dealt with
further severe troubles in the Highlands and Islands, most notably the
land raids at Clashmore in Sutherland on the mainland and Aignish
and Park on Lewis.

Trouble erupted sporadically at Clashmore throughout the year
(1887). The crofters had a deep-seated grievance there since many of
them had been turfed out of their croft lands ten years earlier (on to
inferior land) so that a farm could be formed and let to a tenant farmer. When a sheriff officer came in April to serve summonses for rent

---

[1] A quotation from *The Expostulation* by Isaac Bickerstaffe. It in fact starts "Perhaps it was
right", not "It is all very well".

arrears, the summonses were burned and he was forced to promise on bended knee that he would not return with further summonses. The local policeman subsequently made two attempts to serve summonses on four of those responsible for the deforcing. On the first occasion he was confronted by the wives of the crofters (the men being away at the peats), who burned the writs and threatened him. Only one of those accused of the original deforcement appeared in the Sheriff Court to answer the case. The sheriff (Cheyne) wanted a gunboat and marines to be sent to help the local police force in arresting the other men, and this was reinforced when at his second attempt the local policeman was again deforced and physically assaulted. Cheyne pointed out that Clashmore lay fifty or sixty miles from a railway station, and was more readily accessible from the sea.

Macdonald as Lord Advocate gave his opinion (in June) that the stage of sending a force had not yet been reached. He suggested an effort should first be made to bring the accused to their senses and make them understand if they persisted all chance of being dealt with summarily would soon be over, and the judges, having tried light sentences in vain, would give such a sentence as would put a stop to defiance of the law. He also suggested they should be told that the Queen's Advocate – he added a footnote: "I use the expression 'Queen's Advocate' as being to such people more intelligible and impressive" – had appointed that they are brought to trial and apprehended at whatever cost and whatever force may be necessary. Unless within a fortnight they could present themselves at Dornoch for formal apprehension and examination, the Queen's Advocate could not permit them to be tried summarily, but would have them apprehended and brought to Edinburgh to be tried before the High Court of Justiciary: "Whether effectual or not it seems to me that some proceeding on a warrant for apprehension must take place before an expedition can be sent". This course of action was agreed, and arrangements were set up for sending in troops if the men did not accede.

In November the crofters took the law into their own hands and took possession of Clashmore Farm, driving their cattle onto it, pulling down dykes and burning down the steading. At this point a military expedition was despatched to Assynt, led by a gunboat with a force of police and marines. Notices of Interdict were served and arrests were made.

Macdonald advised Lothian that he had consulted with the sheriff and that three or four of the older Clashmore men could be tried in the High Court in Edinburgh, and the others tried summarily. In the event those who appeared in the High Court were two men and two women. Macdonald as Lord Advocate led the prosecution. He made much play of the fact that the "mob" had blackened their faces and disguised themselves when raiding the farm; in his address to the jury he said the case had distressed him more than any of the others because of this. They had cases before them in which people had assembled in an open and straightforward way to resist and defeat the law, but this was the first time in the history of Scotland that they had heard of people taking such steps when they were going to commit breaches of the law. It was, he said, "a horrible thing to think in our own Highlands, where they had always looked upon the people as high-minded and devoid of meanness, they should have people brought there ... charged with the perpetration of such acts". He claimed that outsiders, who kept themselves out of danger, incited these people "a peaceable population, and so far as one could judge, comfortable in their lives – to acts of violence". Blackening faces plainly indicated the criminality of the proceedings. He ended by saying that "either the Executive must be overborne by a general rebellion, or a small rebellion must be dealt with firmly on the spot". The jury found the two women and one man guilty, and the case against the other man not proven, and gave a strong recommendation to leniency.

The judge, (Lord Craighill), in sentencing those found guilty referred particularly to "unwomanly and degrading acts of the women blackening their faces. Women are probably more subject to the influence of others than men", and he could not believe that "the female prisoners, without being influenced by others, would take the lead in such an affray and would have so disfigured themselves". On that ground he reduced their sentence, although he had very grave doubts about doing so. His pronouncement of a sentence of nine months' imprisonment on each of the women (one of whom had a son of about eighteen months) caused a "sensation in Court". The man was sentenced to twelve months. The sentences do seem harsh – again compare them with, for example, those in the City of Glasgow Bank trial. Not surprisingly there was an outcry over them. At a highly charged meeting of about fifty Highlanders, chiefly from Sutherland, held in Edinburgh following the trial, the chairman attacked the conduct of the

Lord Advocate and the judge. "The Lord Advocate", he said, "was supposed to sympathise with Highlanders", but his conduct in this case
showed his sympathy was very small. His principle seemed to be: "no
case – bully the defence witnesses"; but, he said, the Lord Advocate was
mildness itself compared with Lord Craighill, whose conduct was "the
rankest bullyism they could find in the Cowgate in Edinburgh".

Many of the criticisms were no doubt justified. The authorities, including Macdonald, in their dealings with the situation on the ground,
and in their conduct of this and other trials, too often display a pat-
ronising attitude towards the crofters, regarding them as worthy but
simple, uneducated and therefore gullible peasants. They were regarded as normally law-abiding, honest people led on to criminal acts by
agitators. Because of a fundamental lack of human understanding, in-
sufficient heed was paid to their plight and the need to improve it,
even following the evidence before the Napier Commission. So far as
the legal authorities were concerned, the law had to be enforced, otherwise lawlessness would prevail. At the crofters' trials the juries con-
sistently voiced their sympathy in the only way they could by strongly
recommending leniency, or whenever they possibly could, acquitting.

At the end of 1887 and beginning of 1888 events in Lewis brought
the focus of the legal and political authorities, and of the press, on to
the desperate situation on that island. In particular, two land raids –
one in November at Park deer forest, followed by another at Aignish
– together involving hundreds of men, dramatically drew attention to
the plight of much of the population.

The problem of over-population was particularly acute on Lewis.
In less than a century the population had increased more than three
times. Increasingly people on smaller sub-divided holdings (usually
on inferior land) could eke out a living only by supplementing their
income from some additional source – normally the fishings. When
these failed, as they had done for the past two seasons by the end
of 1887, the survival of many was threatened, even though the crops
had been good. There was a genuine fear of destitution and starvation. Old resentments flared when they saw, for instance, the land at
Park, which had been entirely occupied by crofters until some two
generations earlier, when they had been turned out to poorer areas to
allow the whole district to be turned into a huge sheep farm, now giv-
en over to a deer forest. Pleas to be allowed the use of the land fell

on deaf ears. Lady Matheson, the chief landowner, was unyielding. It was hardly surprising that the men – many of them young cottars – should have taken the action they did. The Park raid had followed a few days after a meeting where the decision was taken to go on to the deer forest and shoot down as many deer as possible. A report of the meeting was sent to Macdonald, who spoke to the sheriff (Cheyne) and passed on to Lord Lothian his view that nothing could be done before the day of the raid except to put the local authorities on the *qui vive*, which had been done. "Probably there is more noise than action in the affair", Macdonald commented. Lothian replied that if it came to anything steps to punish the offenders must be taken at once and, taking no chances, he approved the sending of troops and a gunboat. The War Office was contacted, and Lothian wrote to the Admiralty informing them that the Lord Advocate "who is familiar with the district" had telegramed him that "from geographical difficulties troops will require to be moved generally by sea from one point of Lewis to another. A gunboat is therefore necessary". By the time a detachment of Royal Scots from Glasgow arrived in Stornoway the raid was practically at an end. However, Macdonald advised Lothian that as the expedition had started it would be unwise to make any charge until sufficient arrests were made to vindicate the law. The intention was to make arrests and have trials before Christmas. He hoped "for the sake of the Highland people themselves that the Judges will recognise the lesson of last year's convictions with mild sentences has not produced the results hoped for". A gunboat with marines duly arrived later, followed by another.

The raiders (some 150 of them) camped for two days in the forest, killing a number of deer. The actual number varied greatly according to different accounts: as many as 300 according to a telegram from the Park Estate's Solicitors, but only fifteen to twenty according to the gamekeeper at the trial and as few as three to six according to a telegraphed report from the sheriff immediately following the end of the raid. There was no violence apart from a confrontation in the deer forest between some of the men led by Donald Mackinnon and Sheriff Fraser and the police superintendent; Mackinnon threatened to shoot the sheriff, not recognising who he was; the sheriff read the Riot Act both in Gaelic and English. The intention of the raiders was not to take over the land there and then; it was a demonstration of their need to alleviate their and their families' immediate hunger for food and their lasting need for land.

The law had to be "vindicated". Fourteen were arrested, including Donald MacRae, the schoolmaster, and two other alleged instigators. The military force was not used at all in this connection. The sending of the force provoked an inflammatory letter (dated 26th November 1887) from RP Cunninghame Graham to *The North British Daily Mail*:

> Sir, Military again for the West Highlands. The old Tory dodge. The unfortunate people, and the Tory Government to their cry for meal, answer with bullets. Points for your readers. Are deer game? Have the crofters broken any law? Have they injured any man? Have they destroyed the work of any man's hands? Scotland is a free country – quite, it appears, for a crofter to starve in, or for a deer to eat his crops in. I wish – and surely there is no harm in wishing – that there were not a deer, a grouse or a salmon in all the Highlands. If there were not, we might see more sheep, more agriculture, and more men, and fewer Cockneys and German Princelets.

Macdonald suggested to Lothian that the instigators should be sent to trial by jury and the others ("a poor and ignorant set of people") promptly tried summarily. "This would mean no time for *sensation*". They had, he said, given the criminal authorities no trouble in being apprehended and the injury done had proved trifling. He added: "These are my pretty strongly held views but as *policy* as well as *criminal procedure* requires to be considered in these cases, I shall not act on my own opinion until I hear from you … then within a fortnight of the *émeûte* the actors would be punished, showing swift and merciful justice". Lothian agreed, but in the event only six of the men were tried, including MacRae and two other instigators, all at the High Court in Edinburgh the following month, January 1888.

Macdonald did not take part in the prosecution, which was led by the Solicitor-General, JPB Robertson. The charge was mobbing and rioting, the indictment stating that the prisoners had formed a scheme for trespassing on the Park deer forest and certain of them had instigated and incited others to commit the trespass; fifteen to twenty deer had been killed and others driven off the forest. The object was to intimidate the tenant into giving up his possession. This was the first case of importance in which the new simplified form of indictment introduced by Macdonald's Criminal Procedure Bill in 1887 was used.

The jury did not accept the charge against the accused that they formed part of a riotous mob, despite the firm direction of the judge, Lord Moncrieff, and took less than half an hour to reach a verdict of not guilty against all of them. They were no doubt persuaded by what Lord Moncrieff described as the perfervid eloquence of some of the defence submissions. "This is not a political meeting, but a Court of Law", he said in his address to the jury. "What you have to try is entirely a question of fact". But the jury must have found it impossible not to take into account the human and surrounding circumstances of the prisoners.

Defence Counsel criticised the public prosecutor for bringing the case, and maintained that as it was only a poaching expedition, the charge should have been brought under the Day Trespass Act and dealt with summarily by a JP: if convicted, the accused would be liable to a fine of up to £5. The not guilty verdict was greeted with loud and prolonged cheering, and the schoolmaster Donald MacRae was carried shoulder-high through the streets.

The raid at Aignish, near Stornoway, which followed a few weeks after the Park raid, was one of the most serious of all the disturbances. The intention to raid the farm was openly announced. A large body of some hundreds of men went there and told the tenant farmer that the farm was to be taken over to relieve the starvation of cottars in the district. A few days later at a meeting at the neighbouring churchyard, which it was said the Aignish tenant had desecrated by allowing his stock to graze there at will, it was resolved to enter the farm on 9th January 1888 and drive off the tenant's stock. Macdonald and the other authorities, being forewarned, were able to take steps to counter the raid. A gunboat was moved into the area. A proclamation was posted in many parts of the district warning people not to enter the farm. A force of fourteen police with thirty armed marines moved into the farm building out of sight to await the invasion of the insurgents on the appointed day, and twenty-five soldiers of the Royal Scots moved in to the adjoining farm of Melbost.

Sheriff Fraser, the Chief Superintendent and the Deputy Fiscal joined the force at the farmhouse. A large contingent numbering many hundreds had gathered on the hill overlooking Aignish Farm, and when a body of about fifty of them rushed down on the farm brandishing stocks to drive off the sheep and cattle they were met at the steading by the sheriff and police. The sheriff, speaking in Gaelic, tried to warn the crowd and read the Riot Act, but was unable to continue due to the actions of the crowd. Those not close to the sheriff continued to drive off the stock. He then called up the marines and police and twelve men were arrested after a struggle. The crowd threatened that the party would never succeed in taking their prisoners to Stornoway, and threw stones at the police and marines. The sheriff then sent for the Royal Scots and on their arrival the party started for Stornoway. The crowd began throwing stones, injuring the Depute Fiscal, several soldiers and policemen including the Superintendent, and the soldiers had to charge twice with fixed bayonets to keep the crowd back. Ultimately the twelve arrested were brought to Stornoway. They had to wait only three weeks before being tried in separate batches before Lord Craighill and a jury in the High Court in Edinburgh. The trials started on 30th January, immediately before the Clashmore hearing.

John Macdonald led the prosecution. The case was clearly strong, while the defence had not much to offer and was not helped by claiming that the accused (who pleaded not guilty) had gathered not with criminal intent but to visit the graves of their ancestors in the churchyard. In his address to the jury in the first trial Macdonald laid it on thick: "It was a most lamentable thing that it should have come about in the year 1888 that it should be supposed for a single moment that people, by mobbing and rioting, were going to get rights which they did not at present possess". If that were allowed either "all property must become unsafe, and therefore all prosperity must cease or else tyranny must come in … It was lamentable to see men, who had no doubt borne an irreproachable character hitherto, led into acts, which, if permitted, would be fatal to the existence of society". The case, he said, had "every conceivable element which went to make up lawlessness". He found:

> a touch of humour in the idea that they (the accused) were going to assemble in the Lews a crowd of 700 or 800 people by the signal of a red flag, to shout and yell round the Sheriff, while their only object was to visit the graves of their fathers

… It was perfectly obvious that men intending to visit the graveyard had no need to spread themselves out in a line, so that if they did advance the whole stock of the farm must be driven off.

He concluded:

> It was said some of the men said to Newall (the Aignish tenant) and the Sheriff they were starving … no one would doubt there was a considerable amount of destitution in Lewis. The words "they were starving" no doubt implied what was probably true – that many of them were in a very bad way. But if they were moved by pangs of hunger and the immediate pressure of their families, surely one would have expected their course would have been to act in such a way as if they wanted food. There was no evidence of the immediate requirement of distribution of food. No trace of anything more than that they were looking forward with some doubt and difficulty to the future. What they went to Aignish for was to assert an intention on their part to have a different future before them than had been in the past, and to do that by force and violence.

All three in the first trial were found guilty by the jury who recommended them to leniency.

In his address in the second trial, Macdonald said he hoped the jury would believe him that it was "a painful duty to prosecute poor and ignorant men like these … These prisoners were not the heads; they were the mere instruments, led on by others". He would be only too glad if the jury saw their way in this case also to recommend leniency. This they did, while finding all six guilty.

The three charged in the third trial were also found guilty of mobbing and rioting and driving off the stock, and by a majority the charge of attacking the police and attempting to rescue the prisoners was found not proven. The sentences imposed on the crofters ranged from nine to fifteen months. Lord Craighill said that but for the recommendation of leniency the sentences would have been far heavier, as "the offence was enormous".

The Scotsman reported that the result of the Aignish trial was received with great coolness by the local people and that there was a feeling it would not alter the intention to raid the farm when the spring work commences. More heated responses came from Dr Cameron and other speakers, addressing public meetings, complaining of the injustice of the sentences which, it was said, had "elevated the men sentenced to the rank of political martyrs". At a demonstration in Greenock a resolution was adopted in favour of mitigation of the sentences passed on the Aignish and Clashmore crofters; Professor Lindsay said the Secretary for Scotland and the Lord Advocate had been besieged for some time but had not yet softened their hearts, and Dr Cameron complained of the vindictive manner in which the proceedings were carried out against people who were not ordinary criminals, but hungry men.

What action was the Scottish Office taking? At the end of January 1888 Sheriff Fraser and Malcolm McNeill, appointed by Lord Lothian, presented to him their report on the condition of the cottar population in Lewis. The two made house-to-house visits and convened meetings of the local parochial boards; their report sets out clearly what they describe as "the extreme gravity of the situation", placing it in historical context. They concluded that the crisis was even more acute than that which occurred through the ruin of the kelp industry between 1840-44, and the failure of the potato crop in 1846:

> Actual starvation in the Lews has only been averted during the present winter by the exceptional abundance of last season's crop, and will almost certainly occur before the crop of next season is available; your Lordship (Lothian) will judge whether the immense population here congregated can safely be permitted to rely on a chance so precarious in this climate as a continuance of favourable harvests … the disaster which was averted by the growth of a new industry (the herring fishery) subsequent to 1851 must certainly befall the Lews, and that soon, unless either employment can be found for the inhabitants, or the population is greatly reduced.

In addition the Parochial Boards needed further funding if they were to meet the requirements of relief brought about by "widespread destitution" which from their inquiries Fraser and McNeill regarded as inevitable. "The scale of aliment", they added, "is so low that without an abuse of words it may be called illusory".

A copy of the report was forwarded by Lothian to the Queen. He observed "with great regret the great amount of distress from want of food, overcrowding and miserable conditions of the houses in many parts of the Island". He also reported there had been no fresh outbreaks against the law, and expressed the hope that the Aignish convictions might have a salutary effect. The Queen was anxious to hear of the state of affairs in the Highlands in detail, being most desirous that "the alleviation of misery in which many of her loyal Highlanders are steeped should be done without delay".

Sheriff Fraser continued to send regular reports. On 2nd February he reported that the situation in Lewis was daily becoming more alarming, and government action was required. Petitions arrived from communities there and elsewhere soliciting help to keep the people from starving. Petitioners (155 of them) from Tongue blamed the existing land laws entirely, and said that unless they got instant relief through the supply of work or meal they would be forced "to do things which if we were placed even in the shadow of comfort we would shrink from doing". A letter on behalf of the people of Barvas (Lewis) to Lord Lothian referred to meals received from the Destitution Fund in Stornoway, stated that the people were most willing to do any work to keep themselves alive, and said about 100 men were engaged in making a road to the harbour in the hope of getting a little meal for their work. They asked that the government have a pier constructed at the harbour, saying the people were willing to refund ten percent of their earnings in aid of the cost, and to give up five percent of their fishings catch till the cost is met, and those engaged in the fishings would give ten days free labour. The reluctance (almost inbuilt, it would seem) of the Scottish Office establishment to appreciate the gravity of the situation and the need to take immediate action is indicated by the comments of two senior officials appended to this letter with its constructive suggestions. Dunbar (the under secretary) comments: "some of the people seem prepared to put their shoulders to the wheel" and Cochran Patrick writes: "it (acting on the people's proposals) would be as good as a gunboat for producing a quieting effect". In reply to Sheriff Fraser's urgent recommendations all these two officials would concede was that an advance (not a grant) might have to be made on security of future rates payments. And when the Secretary of the Board of Supervision in Lewis reports two months later that he regarded "the alarm of destitution" as "a sham got up to serve some purpose" (contrary to clear evidence from the board's Inspectorate), Cochran Patrick commented that the letter illustrated "the difficulty of arriving at any satisfactory conclusion in any matter connected with the Highlands and Islands. A good practical rule would seem to be 'not to believe anything you hear and only half of what you see'".

Sir James King, Lord Provost of Glasgow and Chairman of the Relief Committee, wrote to Macdonald after a public meeting that it would be difficult to estimate the money likely to be gathered in Glasgow, as disregard of the law and of rights of property by certain crofters would limit very much the number and scale of contributions. "We know," he wrote, "that the real cure for the prevalent destitution is emigration but in order to carry this out without hardship time and much money will be needed. Probably 14,000 instead of 28,000 would be a population as large as could expect to live in comfort and independence in Lewis. We think the State should furnish such aid as may be necessary in carrying into effect an emigration scheme". He also made the suggestion for work to be done on roads, harbours etc in exchange for daily doles of money or food, and states he will try to get work in the Clyde shipbuilding yards.

Urgent questions were asked in Parliament when it re-convened in February. When there was a full debate on the situation in the Commons Macdonald bore the brunt of the criticism from the Opposition over the government's handling of events, and most strongly over his responsibility as Public Prosecutor for the crofters' trials. Dr Cameron moved an amendment to the Address in Answer to the Queen's Speech regretting that there was no reference in the Speech to the critical state of affairs in the Highlands and Islands, or to any proposed legislation to remedy it. He complained about the government's reliance on gunboats and martial law, and a vigorous enforcement of the law which he claimed was vindictive and one-sided. The Park deer raid was carried out by men driven by extremity to relieve them and their families from starvation; it had been "dealt with by means of gunboats" and the full force of the law, yet the jury found the accused not guilty of the crime of mobbing and rioting. Dr Cameron severely criticised Macdonald for "dragging" the accused to Edinburgh for trial, which meant they could not bring witnesses in their defence as they had no funds, and also for using one of the ringleaders (Donald MacKinnon) in the raid as a prosecution witness to incriminate the others. There was also objection to the law being set in motion by the Procurator Fiscal because he was the law agent of Lady Matheson, the proprietor of the island and also of the tenant of the Deer Forest.[1]

The crofter question would not, Cameron said, be settled by a policy of dragooning. "It was the business of the Government to decide as to the primary and heroic remedies – the alteration of the land laws, the provisions for the cottars, and the schemes of emigration". As always the subject of emigration proved the most emotive of all; Dr Cameron described McNeill's report as "a special plea for emigration from be-ginning to end". Something of the highly charged atmosphere of the debate, and the bitterness of feeling, is shown in his derisive sugges-tion that if the government believed prosperity could be restored by reducing the population they must try "as a much more likely par-allel the plan ironically embodied in his 'Modest Proposal' by Dean Swift".[2] He added: "It was absurd to rely on emigration – in the case of the Highlands – as a remedy, for the very simple reason that the peo-ple would not emigrate. Why? Because traditions lived among them, and there had been some cruel instances of clearances within a gen-eration". If the parts of Lewis used primarily as deer forests and for game – comprising 250 square miles (about half the whole area of the island) – were handed over to the crofters, the island would, he said, be considerably less over-populated.

Another crofter MP, Mr A Sutherland, also attacked the Lord Advo-cate and the government. He referred to the Clashmore disturbances as merely technical law-breaking. Under the Crofters Act it was intended

[1] Throughout the disturbances there were complaints about Procurator Fiscals carrying on private practice, often as agents for the landlords. Macdonald expressed his "decided opin-ion" in the House in 1888 that "no other employment should be held by Procurator Fiscals at all", and if they were allowed any other employment it should be a public appointment and "not connected with the work of the law in any other department or connected with agency for individuals".

[2] Written in 1729, a wicked ironic tract for making poor children "beneficial to the publick" by proposing they should be used to feed the rich.

that all arrears of rent incurred before the Act should be dealt with by the Crofters Commission, but a court decision had allowed landlords to sue for these arrears. Immediately after this defect in the Act was found summonses were issued against the people in arrears at Clashmore. These people, thinking they had the protection of the Commission, and that if they accepted service of the writs they would be deprived of the rights which it was the wish of the House to bestow upon them, resisted such service. The defect in the Crofters Act which had caused the raiders to act in the way they did, resisting payment of arrears of rent, had subsequently been remedied by the government passing an Act to prevent landlords recovering arrears.

Sutherland said the Crofters Acts had failed the crofters in not making proper provision to meet their demands for land. This, and not the problem of rack-renting, was their primary grievance. They wanted to have the land of which they had been deprived in the past given back to them for cultivation; up to the present moment (nineteen months after the passing of the Act) "not a single inch of additional land had been provided for the people under the operation of that Act". Again Macdonald was criticised for the Clashmore accused being "dragged away" to the court in Edinburgh to face a charge of mobbing and rioting, which did not even amount to common assault: "For the putting down of this trivial affair ... all the mighty resources of the Government were called into action".

John Macdonald led the reply on behalf of the government. In a firm, forceful speech lasting one and a half hours he took the House through a narrative of the main events and defended the legal action taken and government policy. On the causes of the troubles he said:

> It (destitution in Lewis) has not arisen from anything connected with the crofts ... It is admitted on all hands that last year's crop was one of the best they have had; and the reason why the present destitution has come upon the crofters is not in consequence, as is said, of their not having sufficient land to cultivate, or of anything connected with the crofts which is abnormal but is entirely in consequence of the absolute failure of the fishing industry ... there was nothing in what took place to indicate to the authorities any immediate, pressing, actual want on the part of the community.

On the relevancy of the charge against the accused in the Park trial he pointed out that the terms of the indictment had not been challenged and the judge had distinctly held that the deer raid was unquestionably an act of mobbing and rioting. Dr Cameron was wrong in saying that he (Macdonald) had failed to bring a relevant indictment. Dr Cameron interrupted to say that the jury found so, but Macdonald pointed out that this was not within the province of the jury, whose duty was to take the judge's statement of the law and then to deal with the facts.

He stated his view that the deer raid was not:

> of so great consequence in itself. Its importance was that it indicated a general lawless tendency among the community in the Island of Lewis, indicating, as it did, an express determination on the part of the people there to override the law – a purpose which I believe would not have entered their minds unless it had been brought to them from without. When such things took place, it was absolutely necessary for the Executive to see that measures should be taken to prevent them occurring again.

The trouble at Aignish Farm, which followed soon after, sprang (as with the deer raid), in Macdonald's view, not directly from starvation. He could, he said, "perfectly understand these men thinking that they were committing a very small breach of moral and civil law, if they were in a state of starvation, going and stealing a sheep or an ox and turning it into food. Although the law would not justify anything of that kind, yet the law would certainly look upon people who were in absolute starvation as in a very different position from people stealing for purposes of gain. Although 700 people came to the farm of Aignish for the purpose of agitation – and that was admittedly their purpose – what was their act? They do not seize any cattle or sheep and take them for the purpose of food; but they proceed to drive them off the farm, and endeavour to drive them into the sea". He referred to the criticism that the authorities were "guilty of a policy of gunboats" in trying to prevent such illegal actions, pointing out that, so far as he and the Executive in Scotland were concerned, it was not a question of policy at all; it was simply a matter of "doing our duty as Executive Officers …

I think it would be a most cruel kindness to these people themselves
to lead them to suppose for a moment that if they show sufficient violence to overcome the resistance of other law-abiding people in the
thinly populated neighbourhood in which they live, that these people
and their property will not be protected". Altogether he described the
raid as "a distinct, deliberate, wilful persistence in riot, in defiance of
the law, in spite of what the law could do by reasonable remonstrance
to prevent it." The threats and physical attacks on the authorities, including the Royal Scots (and a verbal abuse of the Queen) when they
were attempting to carry out the law, and the fact that, when the Royal
Scots turned the cattle back in the direction of the farm after they had
first been driven off, the mob attempted to drive all the stock – 320
sheep and fifty cattle – into the sea, incurred his particular criticism:
"a more persistent and determined attack upon the law has not been
made in the history of this country". He believed the cause which the
Crofter MPs had at heart was "an honest and sincere cause" but it had
"that blot of criminality and illegality cast upon it by those proceedings", and he urged them to repudiate "the folly of the incitements
which are being held out to those people from day to day".

The Clashmore case he regarded as even more serious. What especially disturbed him was the fact that:

> A mob of people came – not as the Aignish people did, with
> warning beforehand and openly – not a large one, but a mob
> every one of whom had their faces blackened that they might
> not be identified. That is a new thing among the Highlanders
> … (it) plainly showed that they were conscious of the crim-
> inality of their action … But it is worse than that. It is bad
> enough that women should actually in the daytime blacken
> their faces before going upon a criminal expedition. But what
> is to be thought of the Highlanders – the men of whom I agree
> with the Hon. Member (Dr Cameron) that they are proud,
> gallant men – themselves dressing up in women's clothes in
> the middle of the day and blackening their faces?

He found such acts demeaning to such men and detracting from
the "manliness and pluck" which he expected Highlanders to ex-
hibit – a recurring phrase. Crimes such as persistent force and dyke

breaking "can be committed in the secret of darkness … they are extremely dangerous because they are mean crimes and they sap out all feeling of morality and honesty in the community in which they exist".

As to the sentences imposed by the courts, he said he deeply regretted that these had to be given, but in the Aignish and Clashmore cases they were:

> absolutely necessary for the purpose of indicating what must be the result of a continuance of such cases. Looking back to the previous history where riots of a similar nature have occurred, I find that the sentences pronounced were very different indeed, much severer sentences having been imposed for less grave offences. But I am glad to think that, with the greater publicity given to sentences in these modern times, happily long sentences are not so absolutely necessary.

He hoped that the sentences would have some effect on the agitators as well as the offenders themselves:

> There are too many agitators in this country and also in another, who go about carrying on an agitation in one district and another, and at the same time taking very good care to keep at the cool end of the poker. They do not themselves run the risk … I only wish some means could be found by which we could get at those who incite these poor people to acts of violence. I hold them to be more guilty than the unfortunate people who commit them.

He believed there was "a general system of terrorism which has been promoted by agitators in the North of Scotland". What had hitherto been "a peaceable, honest and kind community had had introduced into it, by agitators, feelings of malice, hatred and wanton mischief".

What was to be done? Macdonald set out the options viewed from the government side. He said that all attempts to remedy the condition of the people would be "absolutely delusive and futile which does not recognise the fact that the population of Lewis is in excess of what the land will bear". Opposition MPs protested at this, but he insisted that over the past 100 years this had been found by every inquiry and report on the situation. "In the case of Lewis it was recognised 100 years ago that it could not bear an increase of population at a time when there were only 8,000 inhabitants, and when we did not hear of places being converted into deer forests and let off to American sportsmen. In the case of Lochs parish (where the Park deer forest was situated), we find that from 1790 to 1797 it is distinctly stated that there were no lands in the parish that could properly be called arable". The population was now over 27,000. As his party had said when the Crofters Bill of 1886 was before the House, it could not produce at best more than a temporary alleviation and would not solve the difficulties. "The Crofters Act could not make land, and still less could it make land which would respond to labour by producing such fruits as would justify cultivation, or would admit of any family cultivating by its own labour obtaining the means of subsistence. I say this – that if all the land in Lewis were given to the crofters, it would not enable them to live by husbandry. I say, in the second place, even if it did, it would not put off the evil day for any substantial period".

He expounded once again his strong belief in the need for the crofter to supplement his income from some other source. In the last year, he said, the crops were the best for many years, yet: "we have had destitution staring us in the face, because the source from which the people derived that which enabled them to tide over one part of the year – namely, the fishing – failed them, illustrating what has been dinned into the ears of people for years; but they will not take it in, that the crofter is a man who ought to have an industry and some land for purposes of cultivation as well. If you attempt to make farmers of people who have no capital – so that they must obtain their subsistence entirely out of the land they cultivate – the attempt must necessarily result in disastrous failure anywhere; but still more in such barren wastes as many parts of the Highlands, and in places where the climatic conditions are unfavourable to successful agriculture. This is what we urged, and urged in vain, on the House in 1886. The crofter is practically, and ought to be, an allotment holder. Sir J McNeil reported to that effect in 1851. What I and other Hon. Gentlemen urged in vain in 1886 was that the crofter could not be a farmer unless the State was prepared to provide him with capital for the purpose of working the farm." Curiously (to modern ears) he adds: "I do not suppose any

Hon. Gentlemen will propose that, or that if it were proposed it will be accepted"

Macdonald described the problem in money terms, and concluded that on an economic basis of rent "the crofts in Lewis are not, and cannot have been in the past, the means of support to the crofters". In his eyes the proprietors, including Lady Matheson on Lewis, had made many improvements, but because only a fraction of the rents had been received they now lacked the means of making any more. As a result there was not the same expenditure on labour which in the past had "kept the wolf from the door". His view, therefore, was that "fishing or labour of some other kind is absolutely essential … if a successful fishing industry could be established on the West Coast of Scotland, you may solve the question of the difficulty of population in the future. You cannot solve it for the immediate present". He announced in that regard a government scheme to enable fishermen to procure boats and equipment "on very easy terms", and there was a prospect of a large fish-curing industry being established in the West coast of the Highlands which would employ many people. He felt the government had done all that could be reasonably expected in stimulating the fishing industry. He made no mention of improved communication, new piers, harbours, roads.

He ended his speech by dealing further with the question which he believed lay at the root of the problem – the over-population of the area:

> There is only one way of looking at the fact, and that is, that some part of the population should do, as all the populations of the rest of this country do – namely, go to some other place … Love of country is a very proper sentiment; but if it had been carried out in the way proposed in the Highlands, it would have prevented this country from being the great country it is.

In the past Highlanders had gone to all parts of the world and distinguished themselves in all areas of life; he thought there was too much of "mawkish sentimentality" about the question, and it did great harm. The emigration, he said, must be voluntary, but every obstacle was put in the way of this by people who tried to persuade "these unfortunate crofters that they can struggle against economic laws … The Government is willing to entertain any substantial proposals from any number of persons who may desire to emigrate from the congested districts". But he did not give any details. The government's intention was that, where people remove, the part of the croft divided off in the past would be added to it again, so as to provide a proper size of croft. "It is our earnest desire … that the best should be done for an interesting population such as we have in these Western Highlands – so different from those who live in the rest of the country". Poor, wretched, brave, gallant, unfortunate, interesting, different – all words he used to describe his fellow Highlanders, yet his major speech on this occasion, like other speeches of his, betray his inability to appreciate the real human situation of the people. It is surprising that he should be obstinately conservative and unmoving on these issues when he was usually more forward-looking and pragmatic in solving problems and creating solutions. Perhaps if he had lived and moved among the Highlanders and Islanders more than he did, it might have been different.

Macdonald's speech, though forceful and direct, showed the decided lack of detailed proposals on the part of the government, in the face of what they accepted was a continuing grave situation. There was little about economic support, the provision of labour through improving communications, fishings and other works. Even on emigration, no specific scheme. As another Crofter MP, Macdonald Cameron (Wick) put it: "it would cost the country much less to spend money in helping the people to earn an honest livelihood on their native soil than in sending ships and men to coerce them into obedience to iniquitous laws or emigrating them to foreign lands".

Alexander Asher (one time Solicitor-General) for the Liberals gave a more sympathetic and balanced picture of the people and their situation than John Macdonald, and drew the reasoned conclusion, which Macdonald and the Conservatives, in their hardness of head if not of heart, would not accept. Asher said distinguishing these people from Scotsmen on the mainland, they were less intelligent, less well-educated, more grouped together in small communities, and above all, they were much poorer; and those small groups of people have positively only one possession in the world and that was the sympathy and charity of the neighbours amongst whom they lived. It was impossible to read the report of Sheriff Fraser and Mr NcNeill without being struck by the extraordinary extent to which the poor in that locality helped those who were a little poorer; and it was perfectly intelligible that those poor destitute people should have some comfort in the thought that at the last extremity they would always have a share of the little belonging to a neighbour, however poor, and so feel unwilling to renounce that, their last possession, and go abroad amongst strangers upon whom they would have no claim. He sympathised with the feeling which found its origin in that source; but he deeply regretted it. He thought it would be very much better for the people in the West of Scotland themselves, and for the country, if they could only become imbued with the same spirit of enterprise which had sent Scotsmen from other parts of Scotland into the Colonies and elsewhere abroad. But he did not believe that the result would be accomplished by adopting the policy proposed by the Rt. Hon. and learned Lord Advocate, of putting emigration in the front and foreground as the first remedial step for the present condition of the Highlands. It could only be efficaciously and practically adopted when all those portions of the land which the people could occupy with advantage had been made available for them. When, in addition to that, they had the fullest facilities afforded them for the prosecution of the fishing industry at home, then and after that only, would it become expedient to press the emigration theory.

Towards the end of the debate there were complaints from other Scottish Members about the way the government and the Lord Advocate, as representing the Secretary for Scotland, were neglecting "the true and burning question in Scotland, and that Scottish opinions on matters peculiarly Scottish were voted down by overwhelming numbers of English Tories". The possibility of home rule was aired – not for the first time. One Member stated that the government were the most active apostles of home rule in Scotland that he knew of, by the way "they were treating, or rather maltreating, Scotch business".

Scottish Opposition MPs kept up the pressure, and John Macdonald bore the brunt of it in the House. In May 1888 Dr Clark (MP for Caithness) moved the adjournment of the House "for the purpose of calling attention to a definite matter of urgent public importance – namely, the imminent danger to law and order in the Highlands and Islands of Scotland, in consequence of the complete breakdown of the Crofters Act as a remedy for the crofters' grievances and the pressing necessity for remedial legislation". The chief complaint was that there had been not one case of enlargement of a holding under the Act; in face of the need to extend the provisions of the Act, the government appeared to be taking no positive action, and the Lord Advocate in reply to questions had given only curt, negative replies. Macdonald reiterated the arguments about over-population, and quoted his comments on the Bill in 1886, pointing out the need for capital to use and stock the land properly. "This Bill suggested nothing whatever to make it sure that when they had been given this additional pasture land, those who took it would be able to make a beneficial use of it, and give a reasonable return to the person to whom it belonged". He had not seen any change in the situation which had in fact declined considerably over the last two years; the value of agricultural produce was low, every department of commerce had felt the depression, and as a result the annual value of land had fallen by thirty to forty percent. "To set people without means on land at such a time would not improve their position at all". To him the problem should be dealt with by applying "every principle of common sense which rules men in their own affairs … a mere empirical remedy will do no present good; a mere heroic act, though it may give temporary relief, will not do any ultimate good". Emigration/migration remained the prime remedy:

> No doubt these poor people are attached to their glens and cling to them with a love which it is very difficult for us to appreciate. I admire them for it. It is one of the best features of their character, but it is one of those features which, if it is allowed to take an exaggerated position in a man's mind and affections, does an injury not only to his own personal interest, but to the community in which he lives. Surely we are not doing a cruel thing in taking such measures as we can to give these people in the Highlands an inducement to throw aside their dread and horror at leaving their native country and establishing themselves elsewhere – in places where they can form happy and prosperous communities.

As to the danger to law and order, Macdonald said any fears were absolutely groundless. The feeling of agitation was over, and he hoped that the MPs would encourage these people towards emigration. "We hope", he said, "to be able in the course of a year to remove some families who are willing to go, and to set them up in a distant country where they will meet people of their own blood and people of their own particular sentiments and associations". MPs criticised the lack of detailed proposals, and in a debate later in May 1888, complained that the scheme of state emigration (as some called it) was put in hand without the authorisation of the House. In answer to a question, Macdonald had said eighteen families had already started from Lewis for Manitoba – about 100 souls, selected by Malcolm Mc-Neill. He advised that a scheme would be laid before Parliament the next day. "It required an Act of Parliament to grant money in order to help the people to get fishing boats, but it seemed it required no Act of Parliament to deport the population", said one MP, or in the emotive words of another, "to export the population to British Siberia" (ie Canada). Macdonald countered that "if there is not willingness to go, then our scheme falls through"; all who had gone had been willing to go and there had been a need to select because of the large number applying. But he gave very little detail of the amount of grant aid, and did not explain by what authority he had acted – a point made by Dr Cameron: "The Lord Advocate went into all sorts of extraneous matter; he raised a laugh here and a laugh there; but he carefully avoided what was the real matter of which he and his Hon. friends complained". Dr Cameron said he admitted they had "to construe an answer of the Right Hon. and learned Gentleman (the Lord Advocate) as this would be a contentious clause in a Bill", but the Lord Advocate had given a pledge that the emigration scheme would be discussed in the House before any action was taken, and this had not been done. He told them that the Crofters Commission recommended State-aided emigration and that the policy of government was to carry out the Commission's decision. Dr Clark contended that the recommendation only came from "the landlord part of the Commission". So the debate on the vexed question of emigration continued unabated.

Other remedies for the immediate emergency had been put into operation. In April the Cabinet had agreed to make a special grant to the Board of Supervision in Lewis to meet the danger of starvation there, under strict provision as to the expenditure of the money. In the spring and early summer the fishings were very good, conditions improved, and in September the troops were finally withdrawn.

The following year (1889) Lord Lothian, not before time, toured the Highlands and Islands and saw for himself the clear need for economic development. By that time John Macdonald had resigned his seat in Parliament on his appointment as Lord Justice-Clerk. Before that, however, he had once again borne the brunt of criticism as chief government spokesman in the Commons in an acrimonious debate on the conduct of Scottish business. This was in August 1888 at the tail-end of the summer session. Opposition Scottish MPs complained about the handling of Scottish business and the lack of time given to it; the promise of the new Scottish Office set up under the Secretary for Scotland had not been fulfilled. The secretary was in another place and they had no access to him in the Commons; as a result the executive business of Scotland was conducted there by the Lord Advocate, who acted as his mouthpiece (or "whipping boy", as one MP described him), and who, in replying to questions, read out answers prepared for him by the Scottish Office. One MP said the dual arrangement of the Secretary for Scotland and the Lord Advocate reminded him of another one in Japan, "where it was supposed to be necessary to divide the community into two parts, one substantial and visible, like the Right Hon. and learned Lord Advocate, and the other shadowy or unseen like the Secretary for Scotland". It was, he said, "a stretch of charity to speak of the conduct of Scotch affairs". Another MP asked what was the use of having the Lord Advocate in the House when he did not have the information asked for on Scottish affairs, even at times on legal matters. The MP for Elgin and Nairn went so far as to state that the Lord Advocate was "absolutely wasting his time in doing nothing", an accusation hardly borne out by the facts; Macdonald in his time as Lord Advocate had to deal with a very large and varied range of matters, in and out of the House, and as he pointed out in the debate the number of papers coming into the Scottish Office each year had more than doubled in the two years since its inception in 1885, from 3,111 to 6,387.

Another MP (Wallace, Edinburgh East) made the strongest attacks. He repeatedly said he would not speak personally of the Lord Advocate, but the tenor of his speech was often near to abusive, and he was rebuked by the Speaker. He said when he saw the Lord Advocate and the Solicitor-General sitting together the idea of the whale and the sprat of Scottish politics had less occurred to him than that while the

Lord Advocate really did nothing, the Solicitor-General for Scotland was there to see that he did it; in short he was merely the "sweet little cherub that sits up aloft to keep watch o'er the life of poor Jack". He castigated Macdonald for not taking a much stronger line with WH Smith as First Lord of the Treasury for more Scottish legislative time.

What particularly irked Wallace and other Scots was the allocation made by Smith of half a day at the end of the session for debating Scots affairs. Wallace displayed much of the prickliness of the Scots – sometimes near paranoia – in reacting to presumed attitudes of the English, and even the Irish and Welsh in his case, towards Scottish matters. He knew that "they (the Scots) were to a certain extent looked upon as the legitimate laughing stock of the three nationalities. That was very much owing to the action, or rather inaction, of the Secretary for Scotland and the inefficiency of his co-adjutor the Right Hon and learned Lord Advocate." He had heard the other nationalities refer to any Scottish discussion as "a haggis debate". The Scots, he said, "had great pride as a nation in the Rt Hon and learned Lord Advocate personally. They admired the radiant and spacious spectacle of (him) holding the coign of vantage on the Treasury Bench against all the world, like some Incarnate Judgement *in rem*". But how were he and others associated with him and the Scottish nation represented? He referred to "the libels" directed against the Lord Advocate, the Scottish Members and the Scottish nation by "Punch" magazine:

> Instead of recognising the Right Hon and learned Lord Advocate as a Gentleman who was wearing himself to the bone – or as near to the bone as he could get – in the service of his country, they described him as reposing upon the Treasury Bench in adipose indolence, spread out like Milton's Leviathan "Slumbering on the Norway foam, extending many a rood", and in no way occupied about Scottish business, except to turn his back contemptuously on Scottish Members, and to ward off any possibility of getting on to Scottish business. That was the normal English idea, he would not say of the Right Hon and learned Gentleman personally, but of him in relation to the Scottish Members, the Scottish nation and Scottish Business.

These remarks refer to two illustrated articles about Macdonald which appeared in June 1888, One was a satirical piece in *Punch* on how he dealt (or didn't) with questions addressed to him by Scottish Members; after one member "put a wordy question, seeing that so-and-so was so-and-so, and that if so-and-so did not happen, something might occur, would the Lord Advocate see his way to do so-and so? 'No, Sir', growled the Lord Advocate, half rising from the Bench". Urged on by Members behind him, the Member "repeated the question at greater length, with added solemnity. Resumed his seat. All eyes turned on the Lord Advocate. Said never a word. Presently got up and strolled out, presenting his most familiar aspect to Scotch Members". The accompanying sketch shows Macdonald full back-view in short tail-coat, walking out of the Chamber.

The other article appeared in *Vanity Fair* with a Spy cartoon, one of a series on Statesmen. The cartoon shows Macdonald sitting side-on at ease in his place on the Treasury Bench, legs crossed revealing his habitual red socks, and holding his top hat.[1] The description of him includes the remark that "he is able to import flashes of merriment even into a debate on the Crofters Question".

Hanham described him as the "amiable and bumbling 'Jumbo' Macdonald."

Wallace spoke of the notion of home rule for Scotland growing in Scottish minds:

> If they could not get anything done for themselves, they were driven into a position in which they must make a fight for some kind of independence, and they might rely upon it that if Scotland went in for independence at all, it would not be a fractional independence. It would not be a milk and water matter. They were accustomed to stronger drink than that.

There were calls for the establishment of a Standing Committee of Scottish Members, with the Secretary for Scotland in the Cabinet. Campbell-Bannerman said he did not remember a time when there were not complaints about Scottish business, but he had never known it so bad as it was then, nor the feeling about it so strong. The reason, he said,

[1] (See Illustrations)

was simply because of the greatly increased demands on Parliament's time; new rules of procedure allowed primary measures to go through but had "a fatal effect" on secondary ones, and they were driven to one form or other of devolution. "The conduct of the Government and the Right Hon. and learned Lord Advocate was therefore a secondary cause altogether; if the Government continued to refuse the proposal for a Committee of Scottish Members, a body sitting in Scotland must be set up to deal with the business which the Commons was unable to deal with". Others spoke of the "rumble of Home Rule", and complained that with a Tory government in power, "Scotland got nothing".

The only strong defence of Macdonald came from WH Smith, who said that the Lord Advocate had been incessant in his representations to the government to provide better opportunities for the transaction of Scotch business, and that because of the need to proceed with the other business before Parliament, he (Smith) and his colleagues in the government "have been unable to make the arrangements which the Lord Advocate desired".

This was the last major debate in which Macdonald took part before his time as Lord Advocate and MP came to an end on his appointment as Lord Justice-Clerk.

Chapter 10

Macdonald as MP and Lord Advocate

Before the end of the session the Bail (Scotland) Bill, for which Macdonald was responsible, received the Royal Assent. Alterations to the bail provisions had been recommended by a Law Commission, as far back as 1871, and some of the anomalies had been highlighted in the City of Glasgow Bank case. The 1888 Act made all crimes in Scotland bailable except murder and treason and gave a right of appeal to the High Court against a refusal of bail or against the amount of bail imposed.

While the acute problems in the Highlands and Islands dominated Scottish concerns throughout his time in Parliament, there were of course numerous other matters, large and small, with which he was involved. The most important legislation for which he was responsible was the Criminal Procedure (Scotland) Bill of 1887 which simplified and amended procedures in criminal cases and made provision to prevent undue delays in trials. In particular, it made indictment less complex and also provided that important trials should take place under a Judge of the Supreme Court, in the localities where the alleged offences occurred; all Judges of the Court of Session were empowered to conduct criminal as well as civil cases. A further provision was that previous convictions were to be taken into account in sentencing. The Bill was criticised for its inadequacy – for example, in not dealing with the question whether an accused should be allowed, though not compelled, to give evidence on his or her own behalf, nor with the right of the accused to consult an agent immediately on his arrest and before making his declaration. The right of the accused to give evidence was one which Macdonald would have supported. He wrote that there were many occasions, when defending an accused, that his anxiety would have been lessened if the accused could have gone into the witness box and spoken in his defence. He was proud of getting the Bill – all seventy-seven clauses – through the House without any amendments.

He spoke strongly against a proposal for dis-establishment of the Church of Scotland, castigating Gladstone for not giving a clear lead on the subject. In another debate he said that large numbers of Church of Scotland members "wished to see the people united in a common Christianity, and the ecclesiastical strife which had so long broken the peace in their country smoothed away". He supported the insertion in the Infants Bill of right of access of either parent to a child in the custody of one parent – this, he said, would be in line with Scottish law, and from his own experience the exercise of the right often led to reconciliation of parents "who if left to wrangle over the question of access to their children, would probably go on wrangling to the end of their days". He also spoke more than once on education, a subject in which he took a close interest, and an active one as a member of the Board of Education.

On the licensing laws he was, as he said others should be, guided by principles of common sense, holding that "common sense points strongly in this direction that the hour for the closing of public houses and licensed premises of all kinds should be hours reasonably akin to those which are ordinarily adopted in the daily life of the inhabitants of the localities affected". To him 11pm was not too late a closing hour for pubs in, for example, Edinburgh and Glasgow. Behind the scenes, too, he dealt with a wide range of other matters concerning roads, harbours, prisons, schools, the Church, hospitals, in addition to legal cases.

Macdonald did not excel as a politician. Although the arena of the Commons and political debate suited his taste for drama, the substance of the debate did not always engage him. He had undoubted skills as a tactician, bringing to politics the sense of strategy he developed from his very considerable military experience, but these attributes were not so suited to handling political matters in the front line, nor were the skills required of a criminal defence advocate quite the same as those required of a front line politician. He seemed at times to lack sensitivity to the matter at issue, to treat a serious subject too lightly, or in too disinterested a manner. In a letter to his friend, William Blackwood, in March 1886, early in his Parliamentary career, he writes, "I am glad to have got the ear of the Gallery, which is practically everything", and he recounts how he got a good laugh from the whole House. He makes references in his speeches to trying to keep things light, even in debates where this gave the impression of being offhand or deflective. When his interest was not engaged, he would otherwise occupy himself, being someone who could never sit idle; he always had plenty to occupy him. He wrote to Blackwood from the House of Commons in 1887:

> Sitting in this House is sometimes very weary work, and on this Front Bench I have once or twice, utilising the voice of the Speaker who was on his legs as a hum that does not disturb but helps reflection, returned to my early taste for poetry, and the enclosed is one result – the theme being Willie Mure's charming little child of whom I am very fond. Plunket, who is a very cultivated man and well read in English poetry, praises the lines highly. I do not know whether they will suit *Maga*, but I notice you are diversifying her style, most wisely, and perhaps you may like a little lyric of this kind, which my initials may be put to or not as you like.

Again, Macdonald describes in *Fifty Years of It* how he wrote much of his series of papers on military drill entitled *Common Sense on Parade or Drill Without Stays* while sitting on the Opposition benches in 1886. "Here I make a confession", he wrote:

> I got a factitious character in *The House* for close attention when in opposition, as I sat daily on the front opposition Bench and appeared to be taking elaborate notes. The truth is that a large part of my papers were written on my knee in the House, which, to a man who does not intend to listen, is the most quiet place he can find for mental work and writing when he is a Member of Parliament in opposition.

In the early part of his time in Parliament he wrote further articles for *Blackwood's Magazine*. In a letter from Dover House to William Blackwood in January 1886 he asked if he could make more regular contributions:

> I shall be kept here practically throughout the busy part of the year, and not being a chamber counsel and my practice

lying in the evidence and criminal courts, it necessarily goes to pieces. In addition, this being out of office I shall have plenty of time on my hands … my loss being all at the most expensive age, my being both without practice and without office is a rather serious matter. So I want to ask whether, judging by my fleeting contribution to *Maga*, you would give me a more frequent chance of writing. My presence here would give me a closer and keener view of the political horizon … The matter is somewhat vital to me, as I must have work, from my nature, and I must earn something from it from necessity.

He also mentioned that he had been and would be "for long crippled" by having to help his sister and her husband George Borthwick and their large family who had been "practically without bread to put in their mouths". Blackwood immediately replied:

… If I can give you a helping hand I shall be very pleased and I think we may be of mutual service to one another. I shall be very glad to have occasional articles from you on political matters in *Maga* … I cannot bind myself to anything very definite … wishing rather to lessen the number of political articles … I shall be glad to give you the April one … Another thing I would like you to do would be to write confidential letters regarding party tactics as frequently as you conveniently can so that I may keep myself in touch with what is going on in inner Conservative circles. I get similar letters from other contributors but one cannot be too well informed and in your case I shall take your letter into account when sending you the honorarium for your articles.[1]

Macdonald wasted no time before taking up this invitation. In February he wrote the first "informing letter" to Blackwood, reporting "in the strictest confidence", from the Carlton Club in London on a meeting of the party held there. "We were specially warned that all that passed was on honour confidential, but of course that does not mean that you, who have the leading Cons. Mag. (*sic*) to conduct should not

[1] The amount Macdonald was paid for subsequent contributions is not known. He received £20 for a *Maga* article in 1883.

be informed of what is going on". A distinctly loose attitude to confidentiality, particularly from someone in his position. This and the other letters written at that time – five in all between February and April 1886 – give an inside account of the politics and personalities during that uncertain period marked by fluctuations and factions. Like the *Maga* articles he wrote in 1886 and 1887 they are primarily concerned, but in lighter, more spontaneous vein, with attacking Gladstone's Irish home rule policies and Gladstone himself, "that great propagandist", as he describes him. To Macdonald and his fellow Conservatives, the Irish question affected "the very fabric of the State itself"; what was being matured was "not a bill but a revolution" involving the disintegration of the Empire. The proposal to grant home rule and hand over power to Parnell and his "brother agitators, who have openly declared their undying hostility to Great Britain and to all people who are loyal to the Union" was, he wrote, not only an act of cowardice (giving in to threats of murder and plunder etc), but a crime; the social doctrines preached by them were "the most absolute and grinding tyranny over the individual in the name of liberty".

He wrote one further article for the magazine on the Irish issue. Published in March 1887 under the title *The First Move of the Separatists* it dealt with the first three weeks of the new session. With the support of the Liberal Unionists, the Conservative government strengthened its position. Matters reached a climax in the Commons on 17th February when the Parnellites were defeated in a series of votes, which Macdonald called "a turning-point in the great political crisis", and what would be "one of the most remarkable points in history". The Separatists were in a state of "hopeless disintegration".

The *Maga* articles came to a halt following a private letter from WJ Mure (at Dover House) to William Blackwood dated 18th February 1887:

My Dear Bill

I really must beseech you not to tempt the Lord Advocate to write for you while Parliament is sitting. Your telegraph today shows the difficulty you have to get manuscript from him. There are crowds of things that he should do which are put off till this article is done. He won't work out of the office, and in fact this week has had his time out of the office fully taken up in the House. If you value his reputation as a Lord Advocate which will take him <u>all</u> the application possible to keep up you must stop all employment while (as I have said before) Parliament is sitting. He had an excellent speech on Tuesday.

WJ Mure

The MS will be sent today, so he says. This of course is written without his knowledge, so keep it dark.

This is the clearest evidence of Macdonald's propensity to be involved in many, varied activities at one and the same time, and its effect in diverting him at times from the main task in hand. The articles must have taken up much of his time – they are weighty and well-honed. The letters he wrote to Blackwood from London on the political scene have more spontaneity, and in fact show he had considerable prowess as a political correspondent. He was really better suited to sending the 'House of Commons gossip' for which Blackwood continued to ask, than to writing the lengthy articles on political subjects which tend to the ponderous. The letters contain notable cameos of some of the main protagonists in the House; of John Morley, the Liberal Secretary for Ireland, he wrote in 1886:

> (he) will prove a complete failure, except as a jackal to Gladstone. His speeches are a succession of little lectures, each in one sentence, delivered in the style of the Professor of Philosophy who is thinking out elaborately what he is saying as he goes on, his eyes alternately looking at his notes for a new point, and up at a selected point of vacancy over people's heads. He is utterly devoid of humour, and absolutely without light and shade. The manner of a pedant, with the dullness of a doctrinaire.[1]

Later he describes a speech of Morley's as "a striking failure … jerky, ill-judged, solemn, owlish and disconnected, it was a miserable exhibition, the *literate* floundering in attempting to be the orator".

He is especially good on Randolph Churchill, with whom he dined on occasion, seeing him as:

> A leader of men, a thing we have wanted in the House of Commons ever since Disraeli … He has that faculty of power that has made his very extravagances bulk him more in the public eye … He has realised that the enormous democratic constituency must be spoken to in the language it can understand, with an utter disregard of whether the adjectives are suitable for the polished taste of the *haut ton* … He is not perfection, and I doubt not will commit mistakes. But he has attained that hold, that will make even his mistakes have a chance of being accepted as strokes of genius.

In another letter he says: "If he (Churchill) gets ballast – the real ballast of principle – we shall have a leader second to none of this century in my opinion". This was not to be. After a short spell as Chancellor of the Exchequer and Leader of the House of Commons, he resigned in December 1886, and never resumed his political career.

Macdonald enjoyed being at the hub of things – the more things the better – mixing with people involved in a wide range of activities. He mentions in *Life Jottings* the hospitality he enjoyed at the London home of Sir Francis and Lady Jane Jeune, later Lord and Lady St Helier. "Like myself, she came from the Highlands[1], and her kindness to me has been unbounded even down to today. Their house was the salon where the great in politics and art pictorial and literary and dramatic, were gathered together". This was a milieu he relished much more than the day-to-day workings of Parliament and indeed the Scottish Office. Lady Jeune (as she was until her husband's elevation to the peerage in 1905, taking the title Lord St Helier) was a remarkable woman. She became the leading hostess in London. As a contemporary article declared:

> Fortunate were those who visiting London took with them a letter of introduction to Lady Jeune … She more than anybody fused and liberalized London society, leading it out of the ruts of rank and class into a fellowship with art and letters,

[1] She was Susan Mary Elizabeth Stewart-Mackenzie, daughter of Keith William Stewart-Mackenzie (whose lineage went back to the First Baron Seaforth) and Hannah Charlotte Hope-Vere.

and surprising both elements by the results of her tact and magnetism. An introduction to her became a passport to many social privileges ... Nor was she merely a mistress of social arts. It was her privilege to be admitted to conferences of the leaders of public opinion at which no other women were present. Her intellectual and political influence was as great as the charm which made her salon so brilliant.

Thomas Hardy became a close friend and would often stay at her house (first in Wimpole Street, then Harley Street). He called her "the irrepressible Mrs Jeune". Her husband, like Macdonald, was a Conservative MP and became a judge. Oscar Wilde was another attender at what he described as her "brilliant salon". At the time of the Monson murder trial in 1893 (the year before Wilde's imprisonment), presided over by Macdonald, he was lecturing in Edinburgh, and when asked if he cared to attend the trial Wilde replied: "Certainly not. A waste of valuable energy. If Monson is convicted, I shall see all about it in the papers. If he is acquitted, I shall be sure to meet him at Lady Jeune's next dinner party".

More than ten years since he last wrote for *Blackwood's*, Macdonald was moved in 1899 to write about one of the most notorious *causes célèbres* of all time: the Dreyfus Affair. He was outraged by what he called "the scandalous travesty of justice" involving fraudulent military dealings in the highest echelons of the French Ministry of War (up to the Minister of War himself).

Dreyfus, an Army Captain, was accused in 1894 of treason in disclosing defence secrets to the Germans, and was summarily tried at a court martial held in secret. The evidence was flimsy and false – some of it was not disclosed to the defence team, so they were unable to contest it fully. Dreyfus was a Jew and there was a very strong anti-Semitic element in the conduct of the trial and in the public and virulent press reaction. It seems a scapegoat had to be found and this Jew fitted the bill. He was sentenced to life imprisonment in Devil's Island off French Guiana, where he was held in solitary confinement in appalling conditions. If it had not been for the persistent actions of his wife and his brother, Mathieu, Dreyfus would have remained a condemned man. Doubts about the conviction did arise and, quite by chance, a Colonel Picquart discovered the identity of the real author of the treasonable letter to the German Military attachè in Paris, on which the case largely turned. Nobody in authority wanted to believe it and the military took no action. Picquart was moved away from the scene. It did lead, however, to increasing disquiet, and thanks mainly to the efforts of Mathieu, more support. The country was split in two. Emile Zola in January 1898 sent to the newspaper *L'Aurore* his famous letter, *J'Accuse*, addressed to the President of the Republic openly charging the military authorities with conspiring to conceal Dreyfus's wrongful conviction. Zola was maligned from many sides and had to flee into exile in England to avoid prosecution for his stand. Various shady dealings on the part of the Army were revealed, especially the actions of Colonel Henry who forged Dreyfus's handwriting in an incriminating document, and, when this was discovered, committed suicide.

At last in 1899 a second court martial was held; incredibly the court did not grant a reprieve, despite allowing that there were "extenuating circumstances". This was a clearly unsatisfactory judgment, which led to more pressure for a pardon, and at last the government intervened and Dreyfus was pardoned. However, it was not until 1906 that he was finally rehabilitated. He died in 1935, a broken man, but one who kept his dignity to the end.

The affair deeply offended Macdonald's judicial, military and religious principles. In the two articles he wrote for *Blackwood's Magazine* he pulled no punches in criticising those concerned for their (mis)conduct. They were the most outspoken of any of his writings. The first article appeared in June 1899, before the second court-martial hearing; he entitled it *The Negative Ruler of France*. He paints a dire scene:

> Society is at war. Judges accuse other Judges … Officers of rank and important public officials openly charge each other with lying and fraud … Life is made almost unendurable to unoffending citizens for no other reason than that they are Jews, or if not Jews because they demand that a Jew shall have the same justice as a Christian as an infidel … The social fabric is shaken to its foundations. And the cause of all this is Dreyfus, the helpless prisoner on the other side of the world. He is indeed the negative ruler of France … Since he was deported, France has had no tranquillity. Riotous murder, pillage, terrorism, duelling, suicides, public uproar,

forgery, fraud, lying, slander, threatenings, vituperation, out-
rage on individual liberty, scandals in the administration of justice, and countless other evils, have made her a sorry spectacle
to gods and men. And of all this Dreyfus is the negative cause.

He is particularly strong in criticising the "virulent press" with its:

wild vituperation, false accusation, and incentive to violence, of which the watchwords were *A bas les Juifs!* and
Vive l'Armée. Anyone who, however calmly, asked that light
should be thrown on an episode of doubtful legality and justice, was held up to public obloqoy as a traitor forming one of
a "Syndicate of Treason" in the pay of the foreigner, whether
German or English, or bribed by Hebrew gold. A crusade was
proclaimed against all Jews, and any one who suggested that
an officer of the Army other than Dreyfus required to have his
conduct inquired into was at once stigmatised as disloyal to
the Army, and as undeserving of the rights of a citizen.

The second trial induced further outrageous comment; the fudged verdict did not improve the situation. The five Army officers who acted as
judges were in the pocket of their superiors, notably the Minister responsible, General Mercier, the chief instigator of fabricated and false
evidence at the trial. He pronounced with certainty at the start of the
trial, as he did before the first hearing, that Dreyfus was guilty. In Macdonald's words:

Under his generalship of the anti-revision forces, there has
been much mining and sapping underground, and the coun-
ter-mining to defeat it has been difficult and laborious …
Many forgeries and frauds have been engineered to destroy
Dreyfus, General Mercier having been a leading sapper in
laying and trying to fire them.

As Macdonald writes in his second article, *France Today*, published
in October 1899 just after the verdict: "He (Mercier) could drive five
officers of lower rank to decide the issue as he desired. They have done
it. But they have done it in such a way as to make it plain that they had

in the doing (by appending the qualification of 'extenuating circum-stances') to abandon reason and common sense".

The article was started before the conclusion of the trial, so, as he explains in a letter to William Blackwood, with it dragging on he "had to write up France as she stood before the verdict, and of course the verdict made some of it like wine that had been standing uncorked". He is even more scathing in his criticism of the pervading "cynicism, displaying an utter absence of a sense of what justice is ... the terrible departure from principle which marks the action of prominent men in France, military, literary, and political." Macdonald lays into much of the French press with its:

> daily pabulum of falsified news and morally poisonous matter ... served out as mental food to a vast number of Frenchmen, which can have no other effect than to lower moral tone, to rouse the meanest and the basest of passions, and to prepare the way for moral, political, and national disaster in a race which once was great.

He quotes many examples to illustrate this, often strongly anti-Semit-ic. "The enmity to the Jew has assumed the proportions of a crusade". He quotes in particular from one big circulation newspaper describing Dreyfus as "a base Jew with repulsive beard, with lumpy lips, and an elephantine nose ... It is because of this scorpion, of this being almost as much deformed in physique as in *moral*, of this bird of the night with crooked beak and glassy eye, that France has been shaken to her depths for the last two years!"

Blackwood told him in September that the article was not accept-able as it stood and suggested changes in light of "the verdict now known and people's minds dwelling more on it and the manner of pardon to be granted to the victim by reversal of the judgement". He also wrote: "I am glad you expose the French press ... but none the less I think you make too much of it and take the chauvinist hacks too seriously." In Macdonald's view, without a full reversal of the guilty finding Dreyfus still stood as unjustly condemned, albeit he consid-ered honour was restored, as "the civilised world rejects with scorn the judgment of the five, and bids him (Dreyfus) know that he has not endured in vain."

He did not temper his criticism of the state of France, but did allow at the end of his article a conciliatory note, which hardly squares with the tenor of what went before:

> The outburst of indignation, which was natural, and indeed uncontrollable, has led to word and action which must be regretted, and which it is the duty of all who are calm to discourage in every possible way. It is doing a grievous wrong to lay the sin at the door of France, forgetting that the noisy and the base who assume to speak for France are a part – alas! a large part, but still a part only – of a great nation. The best in intellect, in culture, and in honour are free from the shame of this tragic national drama. All men should hope that they may yet bring their countrymen to a better frame of mind, and to this end refrain from all unjust and exasperating generalisation.

He concludes:

> Above all, let the outcry for "boycotting" whether of trade or exhibitions or in social relations, be quenched by the influence of all right-thinking men. A wrong has been done in France, but it will not be made right by other nations proceeding to do evil in turn. France herself will be much more readily led to right the wrong if she learns that the remonstrances which reach her from abroad come from those who heartily desire her good, and use to her the words not of anger and revenge, but of pleading and hearty goodwill.

When sending the article to Blackwood he wrote: "Don't you think Madame Dreyfus should have a copy with the last two pages marked? It must be an immense uplifting to these poor people to know what all the world outside a degraded France thinks of the way in which they (Madame Dreyfus and family) have been treated." In these pages he speaks of the fortitude of Dreyfus, who, "stimulated by the splendid courage of a loving wife, bore unflinchingly the horrors of worse than savage cruelty". There is no record of such a letter being sent.

Chapter 11

Lord Justice-Clerk

John Macdonald was appointed Lord Justice-Clerk on the resignation of Lord Moncrieff in the autumn of 1888, taking the title Lord Kingsburgh after his Skye ancestry. In *Life Jottings* he wrote:

No appointment could have been more congenial to me. Although the Lord Justice-General is of course senior to him in rank, the Lord Justice-Clerk is practically the head of the judicial criminal administration, to whom all official communications from the Secretary for Scotland come, in regard to petitions for reprieve or commutation of sentence. My experience at the bar having been very largely in criminal practice, for many years as defending counsel and later as public prosecutor, I could feel assured that in the criminal department I could give efficient service. As regards the civil department of the work as President of the Second Division (of the Court of Session) I could not feel confident, but rather the reverse. I cannot express my feelings better than in the language of Lord Cockburn on the occasion of his elevation to the Bench. His words in his journal are:

In the management of facts and trials, and the conduct of whatever depends upon mere science and practical business or rational equity, I may do well enough; but I tremble for myself in causes of pure or technical law, especially touching real property.

Such were my feelings, but I had a comfort that he had not

when he wrote those words. His responsibilities had to be faced alone, as long as he was in the Outer House, where to me there was the knowledge that I would have kindly help from others. For which I have ever been grateful.

However, "kindly help" proved scarce, and he did not have an easy passage. The Second Division had been going through a difficult time. Many felt it was aptly named and dispensed second-rate justice; in fact there was a tradition in Parliament House that this had always been so, since the time when the Court of Session was divided into two divisions. In the 1880s dissatisfaction had never been so widely expressed as to the conduct of business and the standard of judgments handed down. According to an article in the *Journal of Jurisprudence* on Lord Moncrieff's retiral, specific complaints were the constant interruptions from and conversation on the Bench, preventing cases from being properly heard, as well as the judges not listening with patience and forming hasty impressions which dominated throughout the hearing. The judges were also accused of applying preconceived views to certain classes of cases, and to legal principles, to such an effect as to shake public confidence.

The situation did not improve under Lord Kingsburgh. As Lord Sands wrote in 1923 in an article in the *Juridical Review* (*Lord Justice-Clerk Macdonald*[1] *and His Edinburgh*):

Macdonald was the most versatile Scotsman of his times. He excelled in many things, but except in the sphere of criminal law he was not deemed a great lawyer, either as a counsel or as a judge. His treatment of matters of fact was admirable, but his handling of law was superficial and perfunctory. This was due perhaps to two reasons. He had an active, powerful mind, but he was deficient in capacity for subtle thinking. He liked to handle the concrete. He shrank from abstract reasoning.

[1] From an early stage this was the title he adopted rather than using that of Lord Kingsburgh. There may have been a conflict, in using the judicial title, with the hereditary Chief of the Macdonalds of Kingsburgh. John Macdonald's descent was not through the male line, but from his great-grandmother. Or it may be that using the title did not accord with the tenets of the Catholic Apostolic Church in which he held a prominent position. The title Lord Kingsburgh does not appear at all in his "*Life Jottings*" or in his "Who's Who" entry.

That was one reason. The other was that he did not take pains to master the law. Not that he was without industry and perseverance. In anything that interested him he had a great deal of both. But he shrank from application in any subject that did not interest him. He would put it aside and be off to his hobby. He would not grudge days devoted to the investigation of the best form of road metal, but he grudged an hour devoted to a question of vesting or conveyancing. It was for this reason that he incurred among lawyers a certain reproach of indolence, which may have been merited as regards this particular subject, but which certainly was not characteristic of him. He was always doing something and doing it strenuously and enthusiastically. But that something was not always the work which lay first to his hand.

Most critically, Macdonald and his colleagues in the Second Division were, according to Lord Macmillan in *A Man of Law's Tale,* "incompatible in temperament and incapable of co-operation". Lord Young and Lord Trayner both possessed great ability, but also had distinct deficiencies as judges. Young had an exceptionally strong personality; "born to lead, and not to follow", he tended to dominate his two colleagues on the Bench. Unconventional in his approach, and disliking long-winded debates, he favoured getting at the equity of a case, and applying common sense as against technicalities and strict legal rules. He often dissented from his fellow judges' stricter application of principles, and with his more acute mind he was inclined to rush the others into a decision, especially in appeal cases. There were many stories about his behaviour on the Bench. It was said, for example, that when his short fuse of patience was exhausted, he would say to the Lord Justice-Clerk: "We've had enough of this for today", and if the Lord Justice-Clerk refused to adjourn, Young spent the rest of the hearing tearing his papers into small pieces. Young also affected broad Scotch at times; he had a pungent humour which too often vented itself during cases before him, and he had a disconcerting habit of interfering, sometimes to drastic effect, with Counsel, and taking the management of cases into his own hands. Sir James Crichton-Browne in his memoirs described him as "a sledge-hammer, dealing blows powerful and direct".

Young was considerably senior to Macdonald: seventeen years older, and with already fourteen years as a judge by 1888. He no doubt resented the younger, less experienced man being made senior to him. There was also the political difference between Young the Liberal and Macdonald the Conservative, and, with the Conservatives in power, Macdonald getting the appointment of Lord Justice-Clerk. Young also had unfulfilled ambitions to be appointed a Lord of Appeal. In his *Memoirs* Lord Salvesen writes:

> There was no question that his (Lord Young's) abilities as a lawyer were far beyond those of the chief who had been imposed upon him, and he made matters as unpleasant for the latter as he possibly could. Lord Kingsburgh, who long survived him, divided his tenure of office into three periods which he described as Hell, Purgatory and Paradise.

Lord Young, who was generally in the minority when there was a division of opinion, compared his position there to that of a "cat in Hell without claws". In a case before the 2nd Division one of the litigants was named Macdonald. "I thought", Lord Young remarked, "that there were no Macdonald's outside Skye". "You will find them all over the world," said the presiding judge, the Lord Justice-Clerk. "Yes, and sometimes in the most unexpected places", Lord Young retorted.

Lord Salvesen recounts that, when asked his opinion of his chief, having regard to the latter's great influence as a military reformer, Young replied: "The lawyers say he's a great soldier, and the soldiers say he's a great lawyer!". Lord Salvesen concludes that, while Young was "head and shoulders" above Macdonald as a lawyer, the latter knew far more of science than any of his colleagues and had "a great store of common sense", and he writes that he would "rather accept his judgment upon facts in a contested case than that of Lord Young". Lord Salvesen was appointed to the Second Division in 1910 and sat with Macdonald for eight or nine years, when he says he "found him a very easy, genial man to get on with. That was the last stage of his judicial experience, which he described as Paradise".

Differences between Young and Macdonald were very probably accentuated by their opposing views – and in Macdonald's case practice – of religion. Young was said to be fond of discussing theology and

theologians, and of quoting his favourite text: "He that doeth righteous-
ness is righteous"; his views on religion were strong and individualistic,
so much so that he did not wear the crosses on his judicial robe which
all judges wore, as is shown in the painting by W Skeoch Cumming of
the Bench and Bar in 1890, depicting Lord President Inglis presiding over
a hearing by the full Bench of thirteen judges with Sir John on his right.
By contrast, Macdonald's faith and his high position in the Catholic Apostolic Church formed an integral part of his life and actions.

The third judge in the Second Division (from 1890) Lord Trayner,
very often gave the leading opinion in difficult cases. He could rapidly discern the relevant factors in a case, which made him impatient at
times with what he thought were untenable or protracted arguments,
and he could be harsh with Counsel pleading before him. In the words
of Lord Salvesen, who married Trayner's eldest daughter, he "had a
gift of cutting repartee which was not relished by his opponents".

The combination of personalities and abilities hardly added up to
an effective, harmonious court. Lord Macmillan wrote: "There were
constant unseemly wrangles not only with the Bar but on the Bench itself, and cases failed to get a fair hearing". There were many decisions
of the court overturned by the House of Lords on appeal, often in cases
of no special difficulty. At times the Lords of Appeal issued severe re-
bukes, in quite unprecedented fashion, regarding the judgments they
were reviewing.

This situation continued for many years. A highly outspoken article, ironically entitled *The Second Division's Progress*, appeared in the
Juridicial Review in 1896. Written by Neil JD Kennedy, an advocate who
later became a professor, then Chairman of the Scottish Land Court,
it did not hold back from castigating the judges in the Division, adding up to a detailed indictment of their performance over the years. Of
Macdonald, Kennedy wrote that he "never, at least when at the Bar,
professed any knowledge (of law)" – true, if criminal law is excluded
– and that "consequently his first impressions as to the law, specially
its application to complicated cases, are not apt to be infallible".

Of Lord Young, Kennedy commented on his great abilities as a
Counsel, but pointed out that:

> Some qualities which make the success of the advocate are often
> the spoiling of the Judge. Sometimes quickness of apprehension

means only hastiness of conclusion. The evil lies in this: what their Lordships cannot see in the twinkling of an eye, is not worth seeing. Why argue a case which has been seen through at a glance? If a case is dry, or uninteresting, or full of details, it does not deserve attention. The arguments of Counsel are superfluous. Counsel in arguing against the pleasure of the Court, or attempting to change first impressions, are truly committing contempt of Court. To listen to reasons or precedents is "a waste of public time".

Litigants felt that their cases were not being properly considered and decided on, and Counsel could not be sure of getting a fair hearing.

He cannot predict what argument they will listen to, or whether they will listen at all. This is a great evil. Liberty of argument is the only, or at least the best, security for a sound judgment. The part of the Bar is quite as important as the part of the Judge. The Bar has just as high a right to be heard as the Judge has to determine ... How can Counsel perform their duty if argument is turned into dialogue in which they play the part of targets or occasional interlocutors? If Counsel is stating the facts, the Court are instantly curious to put legal conundrums; if he is citing precedents, nothing will serve them but the exact age of the most unimportant witness. One often sees an unfortunate Counsel trying to face four questions at once ... But even when the Division has 'amiable intervals', a Counsel is often reduced to the dilemma of either leaving important points unstated and leading cases uncited, or of drawing down thunder and lightning on his devoted head. That the Court are entitled to every deference is conceded, but their title depends on their respecting the independence of the Bar. Nor is this a question of personal privilege; the rights of Counsel are the patrimony of the Bar held in trust for the public, granted as the main guarantee for justice and security.

Matters became so bad that on at least one occasion the Dean of Faculty of Advocates appeared in the Second Division Court bearing the

Faculty baton as a symbolic gesture of protest, signifying the independence of the Bar and the right of Counsel to be properly heard.
This may have had the immediately desired result of the court improving its behaviour, but the learned judges would soon revert to
their old ways. Kennedy did not expect the Faculty to take any more
definite step, but thought that other legal bodies might formally express their dissatisfaction.

It was not until the retirement of Lord Trayner in 1904 and of Lord
Young in 1905 (at the age of 83) that things improved. By that time
Macdonald had retired from his command in the Volunteers ("his hobby", as he called it), which must have enabled him to take a closer part
in the day-to-day business of the Division. As an obituary in the *Scottish Law Review* stated:

> Down to 1905 the judicial position of the Lord Justice-Clerk
> was anything but a bed of roses. With the encouragement
> which more propitious surroundings afforded, he began to
> give himself fair play, and it was a subject of general remark
> that in the closing years of his career he seemed to take a far
> more active and useful part in the business of the Division
> than he had hitherto been accustomed to do.

It is surprising that Macdonald could not take the lead, and as President of the Court exercise control over his colleagues (senior to him
in terms of experience and intellectually superior though Young and
Trayner were), when one considers his experience of command with
the Volunteers. In the same year that he joined the Bench he was
appointed as the first Volunteer Brigadier to command a brigade,
namely the Forth Brigade, consisting of six battalions in all. The order
and discipline he brought to bear in that capacity, with close attention
to detail, were clearly lacking on the Bench when sitting with his two
colleagues. As a judge he excelled when presiding on his own at jury
trials.

The earlier situation in the Second Division raised the whole question of the tenure of judicial office, traditionally based on *ad vitam aut
culpam*, making them virtually irremovable. Kennedy contended that
"if Judges are to care nothing for public opinion, to prefer the distrust
of the whole legal profession to their confidence and esteem, and to

disregard the unwritten but time-honoured standards of judicial duty, the hour for drastic reform will soon strike". He concluded by fancifully contemplating the most drastic possible action, referring to King Alfred, who "in one year hanged forty-four Judges for having vexed the people by unrighteous decisions. That method was effective, if barbaric; and some of us, in our more indignant moments, are inclined to cry, 'Oh, for one hour of Alfred!' ".

The article could hardly have been written in stronger terms. "Murmuring" a judge is a very serious criminal offence in Scotland. Kennedy, as an advocate with his career before him, must have been absolutely sure of his grounds in taking such a bold step. There was much speculation at the time as to how the judges would react; in the event no action was taken. Kennedy later became Chairman of the Land Court.

Even before his official installation as Lord Justice-Clerk, Macdonald had to advise the Secretary for Scotland on the possible commutation of a capital sentence in a murder trial. This was the case of Mary Boyd, a very poor and illiterate woman of 60, who had been found guilty of stabbing to death her granddaughter, an emaciated infant aged two, in Dalry, Ayrshire. The jury's verdict was unanimous, but by a large majority they recommended her to mercy; nevertheless she was sentenced (by Lord Shand) to be hanged. The recommendation to mercy had not reached the Scottish Office, and it was not until Macdonald reported on the case that Lord Lothian as Secretary for Scotland allowed a respite of the execution, with only a few days to go. The sentence was commuted to one of penal servitude for life – severe enough in the pathetic circumstances of the case. Lord Kingsburgh's report on the case was dated 3rd November, the very day he was installed as Lord Justice-Clerk.

He was thus concerned right from the start with the emotive subject of capital punishment, which caused him much anguish over the years. His strong religious beliefs affected him, and he was known on occasions, when judge in a capital case, to go down on his knees in prayer when the jury retired to consider their verdict. It was reported that he made no social engagements while an accused found guilty in a case before him remained under sentence of death.

Within a few months he presided over a murder trial at Inverness, where Hector McDonald was found guilty of killing a widow at Fort

George and sentenced to death; the first such conviction there for fifty years, it caused a considerable stir. The sentence was commuted, which was not the case in the trial of Jessie King at the High Court in Edinburgh in 1889. This case created much controversy at the time. Jessie King was convicted on two charges of murder – one of strangling a boy of about twelve months, and the other of suffocating a girl of about five months. A third charge of strangling another young boy was dropped. These children had been entrusted to her care by their mothers when she answered advertisements for a baby farmer. £3 was paid over by the mother for the first child, and £2 for the second. This was common practice in those days, the children parted with being often the illegitimate offspring of maids or others in household service.

Jessie King had a child of her own, born some months before the murders. It was not clear what had happened to it, but there was a strong suspicion that it had met the same fate as the others. She lived at the time of the murders with her paramour, Thomas Pearson, who answered the advertisements for her, as she was "not good at the pen", as he put it. She was only 27, and Pearson, aged 59, described as "an elderly man of ill-favoured aspect", was a malign influence on her. He was arrested with her when the bodies were discovered in Cheyne Street, Stockbridge, but was set free following her judicial declaration before the trial in which she admitted she had killed the two children, and stated that Pearson knew nothing of what she had done. He then gave evidence for the prosecution, which meant he could not be charged himself. When he was called as a witness there was "a sensation in court". He said she had deceived him over both children, stating that they had each been sent to homes, but she always made objections when he proposed they should visit them. Without Pearson's evidence it is highly doubtful whether a case against Jessie King could have been proven. No evidence was led for the defence, but defence counsel referred to the jury having to consider whether she was not acting under Pearson's influence, and whether they could not return a verdict of culpable homicide. The Lord Justice-Clerk found that there was no evidence to show these acts were committed in a frenzy or in a state of sudden passion; they were deliberate and intentional, and culpable homicide did not apply in such cases.

The jury did not take long to come to a unanimous guilty verdict, and the Lord Justice-Clerk, showing signs of emotion, addressed the prisoner:

> Jessie King – no one who has listened to the evidence at this trial can fail to be satisfied that the jury could come to no other conclusion … Your days are now numbered. Remember that the sentence of this Court, the penalty of the law, relates to this world only. Do, I entreat you, be persuaded not to harden your heart against the world to come. All that you have done can be blotted out, if you will but repent and turn from it. Listen, I beseech you, to the ministrations you will receive; and as you confessed your crimes in your declaration to man, so also confess them to God, and you may be assured of forgiveness. And now it is my sad duty to pronounce the penalty of the law.

He then passed sentence of death, ordaining the prisoner to be conveyed to the prison in Edinburgh, and there on 11th March to be hanged by the neck until she was dead, and her body to be buried within the walls of the prison. "This I pronounce for doom, and may the Lord have mercy on your soul."

As described by William Roughead (who was attending his first major murder trial): "no sooner had his Lordship assumed the black cap than her face became convulsed, and she uttered continuously heartrending groans till, at the last word of the sentence, she was carried down the stairs from the dock to the cells below". He described this as: "the final curtain of that squalid drama. I can hear to this day, on the return of the fatal verdict, the wave of sound vibrate throughout the crowded benches ... and above all the dreadful cries of the doomed woman as she was borne wailing from the bar"; the woman he described in the dock as "the miserable little creature – mean, furtive, shabbily sinister, like a cornered rat".

While in jail awaiting execution Jessie King tried more than once to commit suicide. Her mental condition was inquired into, and she was pronounced sane. Several petitions were lodged on her behalf, but commutation of the sentence was not granted. When she heard this she was greatly distressed, but when on her last morning she walked to the scaffold at Calton Jail she was remarkably calm. She was the last woman to be hanged in Edinburgh. During her last days in jail she handed to her confessor a statement of her guilt; while admitting the justice of her sentence, she as a dying woman solemnly declared that she committed the crimes at the instigation of another. This could only have been Pearson who should by rights have stood in the dock with her. As Roughead wrote: "None who saw the couple in the flesh can have any doubt as to which of them was the predominant partner".

Chapter 12

Two Famous Murder Trials: Goatfell and Ardlamont

In November 1889 Lord Kingsburgh (as Macdonald was then still known) presided over one of the most famous Scottish murder trials: the Goatfell murder. John Watson Laurie (a 25 year-old pattern maker) was charged with the murder in July that year of Edwin Robert Rose at Glen Sannox on the island of Arran. The salient facts of the case were clearly expressed by the Solicitor-General for the prosecution in his address to the jury:

> Two young men went up a hill (Goatfell) together and only one came down. The other was found, after an interval of weeks, with his body horribly mutilated, hidden away among the rocks of the hillside, and with all his portable property removed. The one who came down was seen within a few hours of the time when the death of his friend must have taken place. He returned from the excursion on which they both started, and gave no sign or hint that he had not returned with him. The next morning he left Arran, and resumed his ordinary occupation until the hue and cry began. Then, when it did begin, he took to flight; and, finally, when he was about to be arrested, he attempted to cut his throat.

Laurie and Rose, both on holiday in Rothesay (Laurie under the assumed name of Annandale), met by chance on a day trip to Arran, and agreed to go back there for the week-end and climb Goatfell, which at 2,800 feet forms the high focal point of the island. Laurie booked them into a room in Brodick. Rose had introduced Laurie to two other holiday makers he had met in Rothesay, who also went to Arran for the week-end.

One of them did not take to "Mr Annandale" and warned Rose (a London clerk, who had a different way of life and boasted that he had some wealth) not to associate with him, and not to climb Goatfell with him. Rose did not follow this advice; the two others returned to Rothesay on the Monday, and Laurie and Rose climbed that day to the top of Goatfell. They were seen at the top around 6.25pm, the last sighting of the two together. Three hours later a shepherd saw Laurie, looking exhausted, coming off the hill. A witness spoke of him at the Corrie Hotel just after 10pm. Laurie returned to the lodgings and told the landlady that Rose had to return home to London. Early next morning he left by steamer to Rothesay, without paying his bill, taking with him a black bag belonging to Rose. He stayed on for the rest of the week, then returned to his Glasgow lodgings, again without paying the landlady. During this time he was seen wearing some of Rose's clothes – notably a white yachting cap, and a chocolate and white striped jacket.

When Rose failed to return on the due date from his holiday, his family, becoming increasingly concerned, called the police, and fully a week later one of his brothers went to Arran to help look for him. After over a week of intensive searching Rose's body was found buried beneath a large boulder at the foot of a precipice on Goatfell, his head and face battered and severely mutilated. His pockets had been emptied, and his cap (neatly folded) was found under a stone nearby, his stick at another place, and his waterproof, cut into two pieces, rolled up in a burn in the gully. A warrant was issued for Laurie's arrest on a charge of murder. He had returned to his job in Glasgow, but as soon as news broke of the discovery of Rose's body he went on the run, and a nation-wide hunt started. A rambling letter from Laurie was sent from Liverpool to *The North British Daily Mail*, stating his innocence, followed three weeks later by another to *The Glasgow Herald* from Aberdeen.

It was not until 3rd September, when he had been on the run for over a month, that Laurie was captured near Larkhall after an exciting chase. When found a razor lay beside him and there was a superficial cut to his throat. Cautioned by a policeman he said: "I robbed the man but I didn't murder him".

The trial opened before Macdonald on 8th November 1889, a Friday. The Crown prosecution case was led by the Solicitor-General (Stormonth-Darling QC) and the Defence by the Dean of Faculty (JB Balfour

QC). At the end of the first day – at which point the Prosecution had not completed the presentation of its case – His Lordship made a controversial pronouncement from the Bench: "It is exceedingly desirable that this case should not be carried over Sunday. I wish it to be distinctly understood – and I am sure the jury will be with me – this case must be finished to-morrow night". He gave no reason for this.

The Crown case was that Rose did not meet his death by falling over a cliff, as claimed, but that he was pushed and then struck a series of blows to the head with a large stone, close to the boulder concealing the body. The defence argued that Rose fell from the cliff at a considerable distance from the boulder, and all the injuries were sustained simultaneously in the fall: it would not have been possible for one man to have brought the body over ground from where he fell, which is very rough and stony, to where it was found. Laurie stuck to his statement that he left Rose at the top of Goatfell. But how to explain how and by whom Rose's body was concealed, and who rifled it? Also how various possessions of his were scattered over the gully, including his cap which was folded and put under a stone? Laurie himself, writing to the Secretary for Scotland from prison after sentence, maintained that the whole of his subsequent strange conduct after Rose's fall arose from a feeling of terror lest he should be charged with murder and unable to prove his innocence due to lack of witnesses.

While the evidence built up a strong case against him, it is questionable whether guilt had been proven. It was, in Macdonald's address to the jury "certainly one of the most remarkable cases that have ever come before a Court of Justice". He finished his hour-long charge at 9.40pm on the Saturday, the second day of the trial. The jury returned after forty-five minutes with the vote of guilty by a majority. It transpired that the vote was eight for guilty and seven for not proven. Even with the smallest of majorities there was no recommendation for mercy. William Roughead, who later edited the account of the trial in the *Notable British Trials* series, graphically describes the atmosphere in the court:

No one who witnessed the closing act of this famous trial can forget the impressive character of the scene. Without, in the black November night, a great crowd silently awaited the issue of life and death. The lofty, dimly-lighted court-room, the

candles glimmering in the shadows of the Bench, the imposing presence of the Lord Justice-Clerk in his robes of scarlet
and white, the tiers of tense, expectant faces, and in the dock
the cause and object of it all, that calm, commonplace, re-
spectable figure, the callous and brutal murderer.

The Lord Justice-Clerk donned the black cap and pronounced the sentence of death, showing more than once signs of being emotionally
affected. Laurie turned round in the dock and addressed the crowded
benches: "Ladies and Gentlemen, I am innocent of the charges". The
Lord Justice-Clerk stopped him, telling him: "you cannot be allowed
to address the Court". Laurie was led away and the court rose. It was
10.40pm.

Much disquiet about the outcome of the trial was expressed. The
Secretary for Scotland (Lord Lothian) consulted with the Lord Justice-
Clerk among others as to a possible reprieve. A petition signed by over
130,000 was presented to Lord Lothian, submitting that the sentence of
death should not be carried out, one of the grounds referring to insanity running in Laurie's family, and that he himself "has shown from
infancy decided symptoms of mental aberration, which accounts for
the extraordinary and eccentric character of his conduct subsequent to
the 15th July".

The most damning criticism related to the decision of Macdonald
to confine the hearing to two days. An article in the *Scottish Leader* ten
days after the trial made the point clearly:

> … when men are solemnly contemplating the extinction of
> life this determination to rush matters has an ugly look …
> Fifteen citizens were in durance for two days. They were on
> their own showing but indifferently supplied with food and
> refreshment. Late on Saturday night, when called upon to give
> the verdict, they must have been worn out with the strain, ex-
> citement, and long confinement in bad air. In short, the whole
> conditions were such as to prevent men from bringing their
> faculties into full and vital activity on the evidence regarding
> which they had to form so grave a judgment … fifteen jurymen
> were of jaded minds, and it is not to men in such condition
> that the issue or death should be entrusted.

The paper also makes the point that "it is horrible beyond expression to think that for this man absolute freedom and a criminal's death was determined by the vote of a single fagged-out juryman".

After receiving a report from three Medical Commissioners finding Laurie to be of unsound mind, Lord Lothian commuted the death sentence to penal servitude for life. He would also be influenced by a letter to him from a Dr Robert Bell MD, FFPSG, who had been consulted some time previously by Laurie's family with reference to the mental condition of his sister. He wrote that there was undoubtedly insanity in the family and that Laurie's behaviour in his later years "has always been that of a man of small intellect". The reprieve came two days before the date set for his execution.

It seems in this day and age extraordinary that there was no evidence at the trial of Laurie's mental condition. Over the years in prison his mental state gradually deteriorated, until his death in 1930, over forty years later. Over the last twenty-one years he continued to address a series of petitions and letters to the various Secretaries of State at the time. All protested his innocence, except in one petition in 1901 he stated that he had pushed Rose into the watercourse "and finished the insane action and the life of my companion by throwing several stones at his head". He calls the deed a youthful indiscretion. However, in a later petition in 1901 he retracted the confession.

In 1893 Lord Justice-Clerk Macdonald (as he was then known) presided over – and controversy – than the Goatfell case. This was described in the *Morning Post* as "one of the most mysterious ever brought in any age or country", and came to be known as "The Ardlamont Mystery". Alfred John Monson and Edward Scott were charged with the attempted murder by drowning of Cecil Hambrough, and his murder by shooting the next day at Ardlamont, Argyll, where Monson had taken a seasonal lease of the house and shootings.

The case rested on a chain, or rather, a tangled web, of mainly circumstantial evidence, strong inference and likely motive. Monson, aged 32, was well-educated (Rugby and Oxford) and well-connected. He had experienced a chequered existence, constantly moving from house to (often grand) house for a variety of nefarious reasons, as with a country house in Wiltshire which had burned down shortly after he insured it. He lived a life of high spending, mostly on credit.

In 1899 Monson met Major Dudley Hambrough. The Major, life-tenant of the wealthy Hambrough estates, was in some financial difficulty through overspending. His son, the 20 year old heir Cecil Hambrough, was to follow his father into the army, and Monson was engaged as his tutor for the entrance exams. Hambrough quickly fell under his spell and moved with Monson and family to Riseley Hall, Yorkshire, where they continued to live the high life (despite Monson having recently been declared bankrupt).

Monson's master plan was to get his hands on the Hambrough estates, keeping control of Hambrough, who on becoming 21 could have commanded a large sum for his interest. A London "financial agent" cum money-lender, Beresford Loftus Tottenham, and another London character, Arthur James Jerningham, were supporting him in this. Indeed, it was through 'Tot' that Monson first met the Major. However, Monson and the Major fell out over Monson enrolling Hambrough into the Yorkshire Militia instead of the Hampshire. He had also begun to have suspicions about Monson's financial dealings, and he wished the boy to have nothing more to do with him. Hambrough, at this point completely under Monson's control, refused to return to his father, no doubt preferring the finer life style he enjoyed with Monson.

True to form, his debts catching up with him, Monson and his entourage had to leave Riseley Hall. He took a lease of Ardlamont House and shootings on the shore of the Clyde – in name of Jerningham. Tottenham advanced the money to enable Monson to move north with his family and retinue of servants, plus Cecil Hambrough. When he arrived at Ardlamont, Monson had no more than half-a-crown in his pocket, but he had no difficulty in obtaining credit locally, giving every appearance of a well-to-do gentleman. He let it be known that he intended to buy the Ardlamont Estate, and one of his first acts on arrival was to buy a steam yacht, the Alert, moored nearby at Tighnabruich, for which he never paid.

As soon as he had moved into Ardlamont House he set about trying to have Hambrough's life insured for the sum of £50,000, the policy to be taken in his wife's name. He gave different stories to two Insurance Companies, who both turned him down as they were not satisfied with the explanation of Mrs Monson's interest in Hambrough's life.

Not to be outdone, Monson went to the Glasgow office of the Mutual Assurance Company of New York with another false proposal. He said he was the guardian of Hambrough who was coming into a fortune, and that Hambrough was buying Ardlamont Estate, towards which his wife was advancing £20,000. He proposed to have Hambrough's life insured for £20,000. The insurance company manager agreed and two policies of £10,000 each were issued in name of Hambrough. They were assigned to Mrs Monson in security for all liabilities incurred by her on his behalf, and the first premium was paid by Monson from money he had received from Tottenham, to whom he had stated that £1,250 was required as the deposit for the purchase of Ardlamont (he claimed to be buying Ardlamont for Hambrough at the price of £50,000. It transpired later that the actual asking price for the estate was £80,000 and the selling agents said they would never have accepted such a lower figure).

At this precise point – 8th August – there appeared on the scene another shady London acquaintance of Monson's, a bookie's clerk named variously Edward Sweeney, or Davis, or Scott. He was represented by Monson as a marine engineer who was to check the boiler and engine of the yacht. The stage was set and the players assembled for the extraordinary dramas immediately to unfold.

The first dramatic event occurred late on the night of 8th August. Monson and Hambrough went out in a boat splash-net fishing in Ardlamont Bay between 11pm and 1am. They were accompanied by Scott who, however, stayed on shore beside a second boat Monson had hired that day. This, the prosecution alleged, was in case rescue was required This boat had a plug-hole in it, closed by a cork. The one which they went out in that night did not – that is, until earlier that day, when Scott was seen to be working with a knife on it. It was alleged later he was making a hole similar to the one on the newly hired boat. When some way out in the bay Monson removed the cork from the plug-hole, the boat filled with water and overturned. Somehow or other they both got ashore, although, as Monson knew, Hambrough could not swim. According to Monson:

> Hambrough took off his coat and rowed, while I busied myself preparing the nets … suddenly there was a bump, and the boat tilted and I fell over the side. At the same time the boat capsized, and for a minute or two I was entangled in the nets.

> Immediately on getting clear I called out for Hambrough, and
> then saw him sitting on the rock laughing.

One question mark over this account was that there were apparently
no rocks in this part of the bay. The Solicitor-General in his address to
the jury asserted that the boat must have filled with water much earlier than expected and Hambrough was able to scramble to the shore.
Hambrough had no suspicion that anything other than an accident
had occurred, and he and Monson celebrated their survival over a few
drams before retiring for the night.

The next day dawned wet and stormy. Undeterred by the mid-
night escapade, the trio of Monson, Hambrough and Scott went out
at 6.30am for some rabbit-shooting in the woods by the house. Monson and Hambrough both carried guns. According to Monson, he had
taken the west side of the wood, and Hambrough the east along a turf
dyke; Scott had walked between them carrying the rabbits. After a few
minutes Monson said he and Scott heard a shot; shortly afterwards
they came across Hambrough's lifeless body lying in the ditch at the
foot of the turf dyke, his gun lying at his side. To all appearances he,
who was known to be careless in his handling of guns, had accidentally shot himself while negotiating the dyke. They had, he said, lifted the
body and placed it on top of the dyke, then went back to the house and
reported the accident. They took the two guns with them, removed
the remaining cartridges and cleaned the guns. The local GP, Dr Macmillan, was called in. Having examined the body and the scene of the
"accident", and heard Monson's description of what happened, he
wrote a report to the Procurator Fiscal stating that the death must have
been accidental. Hambrough, while walking along the top of the dyke,
must have tripped, the gun had gone off and he was shot in the head,
dying almost instantly.

The Procurator Fiscal in Inveraray, having read Dr Macmillan's report, had taken no steps towards investigating a possible crime. This
changed as a result of an extraordinary meeting with Monson at the
Procurator Fiscal's office on 23rd August. As the Solicitor-General asserted in his address to the jury:

> Monson, believing that the danger was passed, that the time
> had arrived when the fruits of villainy might be reaped,

invited an interview at Inveraray with the Procurator Fiscal, accompanied by the two agents of the insurance company and his friend Mr Tottenham, for the purpose of securing what, placed side by side with the doctor's report, would have the effect of the fulfilment of this dastardly design, namely the payment of the sum in the £20,000 policies.

A crucial part of the Crown evidence was that Hambrough was shot with a cartridge containing No 5 shot discharged from a 12-bore gun. Normally this was carried by Monson, while Hambrough carried "a boy's weapon", a short-barreled 20-bore gun. The cartridge of the kind that killed Hambrough could be fired only from the 12-bore. A wad of a 12-bore cartridge was even found near the body. The Ardlamont keeper, Mr Lamont, also stated that on the fateful morning Monson requested the 20-bore gun for Hambrough. Monson at first maintained that the shooting came from this gun, but when the Procurator Fiscal made his investigation into the case he changed his story, saying that there had been an exchange of guns, and the accident was caused by the 12-bore carried that morning by Hambrough.

After the meeting at Inveraray full official inquiries were instituted, suspicions having been aroused in particular by the insurance claim, the inconsistent statements about the guns, and the boat accident. Dr Macmillan made an additional report stating that he now considered the fatal injury could not have been caused in the way he originally thought. He had accepted the original statements of Monson and Scott as true, not thinking at that time there could be any motive.

Monson was arrested on 30th August and charged with the murder. Scott, who had done a bunk on the day of Hambrough's death, was also charged in the indictment which read:

> That Monson and he, having formed the design of causing the death by drowning … did, in execution thereof, bore, or cause to be bored, in the side of a boat … a hole, and having plugged or closed said hole, you, Alfred John Monson did in Ardlamont Bay … while the said boat was in deep water, remove or cause to be removed, the plug from said hole, and admit the water into, and did sink said boat, whereby the said … Hambrough was thrown into the sea, and you (Monson

and Scott) did thus attempt to murder him, and that on 10th August … you did shoot the said … Hambrough and kill him, and did thus murder him, and you, Edward Sweeney, alias Davis, alias Scott, being conscious of your guilt, … did abscond and flee from justice.

When the case was called in court, Scott having failed to appear, a sentence of "outlawry" was pronounced against him. He did not resurface until many months after the trial.

The trial opened on 12th December and lasted ten days, an unusually long time in those days. It attracted great public interest – more, it is said, even than the Burke and Hare and Madeleine Smith cases.

The Solicitor-General, leading the prosecution case, went through each piece of evidence in his address to the jury. The opinion of the medical witnesses for the Crown (with Dr Littlejohn and Dr Joseph Bell – the prototype of Sherlock Holmes – in the team) showed, he said, that the wounds could not possibly have been self-inflicted or accidental. It all built up a seemingly damning case against the accused. He concluded that, placing the various strands side by side, the jury must "consider whether the circumstances do not infallibly and inevitably lead to one result, connecting the prisoner with the crimes with which he is charged".

Monson's guilt did seem certain. How did it happen that at the end of the trial the jury gave an emphatic verdict of not proven? This sprang largely from the brilliant address to the jury by Comrie Thomson, Senior Counsel for the Defence, and from the Lord Justice-Clerk's summing-up. Thomson, described as "silver-haired and golden-voiced", was the leading jury pleader of that time.[1] In casting doubt on the main contentions of the prosecution case, he drew alternative inferences from the tangle of conjectural, confusing evidence. Would the boating incident have been a likely means of causing Hambrough's death? He was not at all alerted to the possibility of Monson wanting to get rid of him; he went out the next morning on the shooting expedition without a qualm. On the question of motive, so far as the life policies

[1] At one point he quoted as an authority from his Lordship's book on the criminal law of Scotland. The Lord Justice-Clerk pointed out that no one is an authority until they are dead, and the Advocate remarked: "Well, I hope it will be a long time before you are an authority in that sense".

were concerned, Monson must have known that they came into effect only when Hambrough came of age 21, so it was essential that he
should live till then. As so often the forensic/medical evidence proved
contradictory; the defence claimed that from the nature of the wound
to Hambrough's head - the lack of separate pellet marks due to the
shot not having had time to spread - it was clear that the shot was fired
from a distance of not more than twelve inches. As such Hambrough
must have shot himself accidentally. He was well-known to be careless in his handling of guns. There were other uncertainties, including
the question of Scott's role in these events. Nothing had been proved
against him, and he remained a shadowy figure.

As Comrie Thomson put it at the end of his address: "have I not
demonstrated that there is ample room for entertaining serious doubt?"
The Lord Justice-Clerk in his charge to the jury certainly tended to support this view; this placed question-marks against the main claims of
the Crown's case, and was widely regarded as favouring the defence.
His vast experience as Criminal Defence Counsel, pointing out the deficiencies and uncertainties in the prosecution case, no doubt came into
play. At the end he stressed the need for the jury to have a clear path
to go on:

> You should neither walk through darkness at any point of
> it, nor leap over anything that you meet in it. It must
> be a straight path, and a path on which you have light
> … if there is any darkness or dimness on that path which
> you cannot clear away, you cannot go on to the end. If there
> is any obstruction on that path you have to stop there. The
> prisoner is entitled to that…you must not allow yourselves
> to be urged forward along that path blindly by any demon
> pushing you from behind, telling you that the prisoner is
> a bad man, a liar, a cheat, and that, therefore, you should
> send him to his doom.

The jury's verdict of not proven followed, it would seem, almost inevitably. One juryman told *The Scotsman* that the verdict was unanimous;
after the summing-up, he said, the jury had no alternative, but he added that most of them had a distinct doubt all along. Another juryman
confirmed this. The seeming slant of the summing-up provoked much

criticism in the press. One paper described it as being "generally regarded as a masterly address for the defence".

In *Life Jottings* Macdonald wrote of his doubts about the case, which he referred to as:

> the longest and most protracted inquiry since I joined the profession. I went through nine days of anxiety such as I had never experienced before or since. The case was one which so bristled with points, that one had to watch its course from moment to moment, and to take scrupulous care lest the jury should be misled by feelings roused by the disclosure of the evil character of the accused. So dominant was the anxiety, that morning after morning I awoke long before my usual time, and lay in a dull perspiration, turning things over and over, endeavouring to weigh them and determine their weight in the balance … It was all the more trying because I felt quite unable to form a determined opinion in my own mind. The way never seemed to me clear. In the end I was able to feel that I had done my best to put the case in a fair light before the jury, and can freely say that the verdict they returned was that which in all the circumstances was the safe one … This trial was, in my judgment, the most severe strain I have ever undergone, and not one or two nights of quiet repose were sufficient to restore mind and body … I cannot but be grateful for the freedom during many years from any similar experience.

Years after the case he was reported to have concluded that Monson was certainly guilty. The problem was the lack of definite proof.[1]

Subsequently Monson was involved in a number of cases in the English courts, including an action of libel against Tussaud's for exhibiting his effigy, which he won, but lost on appeal, and an action of divorce against his wife (which was dismissed), one of the grounds being her alleged adultery with Cecil Hambrough. There was a criminal

---

[1] Years later – in 1934 – William Roughead who attended the trial and wrote an account of it, received a letter from a man whose wife knew Monson's mother at the time of the trial. She said that Mrs Monson "was of the same school of thought as 'dear Tot (Tottenham)', openly saying : 'There is no doubt my boy did it'".

action against Tottenham, who was gaoled for fraudulently selling some furniture belonging to Monson. In 1898 Monson was convicted at the Old Bailey with two others for conspiring to defraud the Norwich Union Assurance Company. He was sentenced to five years' penal servitude. Monson even wrote a pamphlet entitled *The Ardlamont Mystery Solved*, which was largely an attack on Scottish criminal procedure. He claimed that if the "accident" to Cecil Hambrough had taken place in England he would never have been accused of killing him.

As for the elusive Edward Sweeney (alias Scott), he re-surfaced in Scotland some months after the trial. He presented a petition in Edinburgh for the recall of the sentence of "fugitation and outlawry" against him. This came before Lord Justice-Clerk Macdonald and two other judges. It was not opposed by the Crown, and their Lordships had no option but to grant the petition, thus not only ending his status as an outlaw, but also removing the charge of murder against him. Macdonald severely criticised the Crown for not appearing and stating their position.

During the rest of his time on the Bench he did not preside over another major capital case. He retired as Lord Justice-Clerk in 1915 when he was approaching his 80th year. He could look back on twenty-seven years on the Bench, years of very mixed judicial achievement. In the last decade at any rate he enjoyed greater authority and success.

Chapter 13

Heaven-born Soldier

The most consuming and abiding interest in Macdonald's life was his close involvement with the Army Volunteers – his "hobby", as he called it, but it was far more than that. He gives a very full account of this in *Fifty Years of It: The Experiences and Struggles of a Volunteer of 1859*, published by Blackwood in 1909, more self-revealing than most of his various writings. Soldiering was in his blood, as we have seen, and he was tireless in pursuing reforms of outmoded systems of drill and manoeuvres. He was dubbed "The Heaven-born Soldier."

When the Volunteer Force was set up in 1859 as an auxiliary force for national defence, he joined the Advocates Company, while still a bar intrant. He describes the advocates drilling in Parliament Hall, at the law courts, often wearing their wigs and white ties. He was soon made a Sergeant ("the first Sergeant of the first corps in Scotland") and was "the first Volunteer the Queen ever saw on parade". He became a Captain of one of the Artisan Companies that were formed. In 1860 the first Queen's Review of the Scottish Volunteers took place in Holyrood Park, with over 21,000 on parade. The following year he was appointed Major in command of a battalion; he was only 24, and many of the officers under him were his seniors. In 1864 he was commissioned Lt Colonel in the Queen's Rifle Volunteer Brigade (known as "the Blacks" on account of their uniform). The Volunteer Force was well established and a capitation grant was introduced. Numbers, however, had fallen off steeply among the leisured and the well-to-do. As he wrote:

"The wealthy curled darlings of our nation" being accustomed to take 'thae idle games of football and golf' and cricket and shooting etc. etc. not as recreations to enliven a life given to

work, but as the business of life itself, it soon becomes impossible to make a sacrifice of a dinner party, or a day's shooting,
or racing, or other amusement, to do a real thing.

He maintained that without the support of the working class members
the force might have died out. He found it particularly disappointing
that the Advocates Company was "the first to die of atrophy".

During his time as Solicitor-General he retired from the Volunteers
as he felt, with his official and electioneering work, that he could not
devote the time he would wish to them. This did not prevent him taking part in the second Royal Review of Scottish Volunteers in 1881,
held at the Queen's Park beside Holyrood Palace in Edinburgh. He was
appointed *aide-de-camp* to the commanding officer of a brigade which
included his own corps. This has gone down in history as "the Wet
Review". There were over 40,000 of all ranks present, stretching in
columns for three quarters of a mile, all in position by twelve noon,
the original start-time. The Queen, however, had wished the review
to be held later – at 2.30pm – because a few weeks earlier at the Royal
Review at Windsor there had been many cases of sunstroke from the
intense mid-day sun.

As he describes in *Life Jottings*:

> Most unfortunately her very kindness led to her Volunteers
> being exposed to a very different evil from that which she
> dreaded. Up to two o'clock the weather, though gloomy, was
> not wet, and had the Review been held before noon, it would
> have been finished before the storm burst. As it was, it broke
> out with fury about half an hour before the time appointed.
> No ordinary words can describe that downpour … the water
> came down like "pipe-stems". There had been nothing seen
> in the Queen's Park to compare with it within the memory
> of man, and the parade-ground became a sea of mud before
> the march past began. About thirty paces from Her Majesty's
> carriage the troops marched through a running stream high
> up above their ankles, which had the curling wavelets on the
> surface that one sees in a swift-flowing millrace. So frightful
> was the soaking power, that long before a third of the bat-
> talions had passed the royal standard, the vast crowd on the

hill surged down for home, and it was with great difficulty that they were held back by cavalry, while the Volunteers
dribbled through the space between the Palace garden wall
and the crowd from the hill, making their way in twos and
threes through the lane kept by the troopers, and doubling
into position as they reached the open part of the Park. One
good came out of this evil. It was a very crucial test of discipline, and that so many thousand men, soaked to the skin,
were successfully kept in hand, recovered from the breaking
of their ranks, and marched past successfully, and were afterwards carried to their homes, many of them having to travel
hundreds of miles in their drenched clothing, without their
being any serious failure in good conduct, led many military
men to form a much higher opinion of the Volunteer than
they had ever entertained before. There were, it was reported,
two hundred deaths traceable to what was gone through on
that day.

Queen Victoria insisted on her carriage not being closed during the parade, and, in Macdonald's words:

Her trusty servant, John Brown, whenever he saw the rain
streaming down, raided the quarters of the maids of honour
and the ladies' maids of the royal party, and carried off an
armful of umbrellas, to the number, it was said, of thirteen.
He took them with him in the rumble of the Queen's carriage,
and whenever the pelting of the storm caused an umbrella to
leak, he handed a dry one over the back of the carriage. I have
no doubt the whole thirteen were used, and that he wished he
had more. What the maids of honour and other maids said to
one another, and said to John Brown, history does not relate.

By this time the Conservatives had lost a General Election. Macdonald
had unsuccessfully contested an Edinburgh seat and he had demit-
ted official military office. He was persuaded to return to the QRVB
as Colonel Commandant and in 1888 was given charge of the newly
formed Forth Brigade; the first non-regular military man to be so honoured, he held the rank of Brigadier-General until his retirement in

1901 at the age of 65. The brigade initially covered a very large area from the Lothians to Perthshire and Stirlingshire, the largest in the kingdom, comprising over 2,500 men. After two years it was split up and his part limited to four corps, including his own Blacks, and still amounting to six battalions.

Many from his Volunteer Brigade, including his mounted contingent, went to the Boer War, serving with the Royal Scots; he offered to serve in any capacity himself, but was turned down on account of his age. Before embarking for South Africa the men went to a special camp. Macdonald joined them whenever possible. As he says, he "had to be judicial in the morning, and martial in the afternoon. It was *toga* in the morning and *arma* in the afternoon." Military and quasi-military involvement did not altogether cease; he was made Hon. Colonel of the Motor Volunteer Corps, which became the Army Motor Reserve. A contingent of cars took part in the King's Review of 1905 at Holyrood, and he had great pleasure and pride in heading the drive of cars, being "the first motor reservist that had ever marched past the Sovereign".

Although no great rifle-shot himself, he took a keen interest in rifle-shooting. Early on in his Volunteer career he studied for and obtained the appointment of musketry instructor, and taught his company musketry as well as training them in drill. He captained the Scottish team which for three successive years won against the English at the annual shooting contest at Wimbledon. "The Blacks" won many team competitions and individually the Scottish championship; one was Queen's prizeman (the highest honour) in 1873 and three others in later years. In *Fifty Years of It* he says there was "much good-humoured grumbling in the Wimbledon camp at the way in which the Scottish rifle-shots carried off prizes", and he tells the story of being shaved, as he lay in bed in the camp, where he had been accommodated for the night by the quartermaster of the English contingent ("the Victorias"):

> Just as he (the barber) had me by the nose and was working about in the neighbourhood of my jugular vein, he said, supposing me to be a member of the Victorias, and by way of being pleasant, "Terrible, sir, a'int it, that so many things is being carried off by thim Scotch?" I held my countenance and saved my jugular, but it was a near thing.

His last Counsel's fee, before his elevation to the Bench, was paid to him at a mock trial at a Wimbledon National Rifle Association gathering, in the form of a kiss from the young lady he successfully represented. "Needless to say", he writes, "on that occasion my clerk got no fee".[1]

In 1876 he captained the British team in the International rifle-shooting competition at the U.S. Centenary Exhibition in Philadelphia. He had special pleasure in his old school in 1911 winning the Ashburton Shield at Bisley (shot for each year by teams from public schools throughout Britain), and as Chairman of the Edinburgh Academy Directors welcoming the victorious team on its return to the school. It was a double first – the first appearance there of the Academy, and the first Scottish school to win the Shield.

By far his most important achievements in the military field were the reforms of drill, training and tactics which were brought about by his persistent efforts over many years – "My 30 Years' War", he calls it, though some of the innovations took even longer. At an early stage he became concerned with the need for radical reforms of infantry training. "It began to dawn on me that the natural conservatism of our race was causing us to jog on with what had served in the past, without sufficient attention being paid to changing conditions … Army officers … had an engrained hatred of innovations." (*Fifty Years of It*). He wanted training by drill and exercises to be on a more practical basis – *relatif à la guerre* in Guibert's words – not confined to the useless worship of external forms, "drill-gone-mad" performed by "unthinking automata", but having regard to the human element within, and to the fact that modern armies consist of men of developed intelligence. He made a detailed study of the leading German and French as well as English authorities, and pursued his campaign with the characteristic thoroughness and perseverance he showed when his interest was so aroused. He saw himself as a pioneer "endeavouring to hack his way through the impenetrable scrub which surrounds the zereba of unreasoning military conservatism", trying to get the War Office, with its "ophthalmia of the official eye", to move from its deeply entrenched position.

The struggle took place on many fronts, but the main changes he fought for (often with the improvement of the soldiers' physical health

---

[1] Normally this would be a percentage of the fee.

as a primary concern)[1] were: the scrapping of "touch" drill and non-swinging of the arms, and introducing a freer air space for soldiers by allowing thirty inches between them; command by signals rather than words; cutting the waste of time hanging about on parade; a system allowing a looser movement in fours in the field and more open formation in attack (one of the more important reforms). Much of this appears elementary in modern times, but such reforms were then of crucial importance in adopting a more suitable and at the same time flexible approach. He cites a vivid illustration of the consequences of sticking to engrained, obsolete methods, in quoting in *Fifty Years of It* the account given by a Boer of a disastrous British assault at the battle of Laing's Nek:

> The red-jackets left their white tents in the morning, after they had had their breakfast, and formed up. Their red coats could be seen by every one, their bayonets glittering in the sunshine. The surveyors went and measured out spots where they had to stand in line; and then they formed up every man straight. The adjutant came and cocked his eye down along the ranks to see that no one was an inch behind the others. They numbered. The colonel rode up. He was on a fine horse, and had a beautiful sabretasche. "Men", said he, "you see those rocks; the enemy is behind them. You are to go and drive them out." They all marched up in rows. All this time we were sitting quietly smoking. As they got near the commandant called out, "Men, defend yourselves." Then we put our gun muzzles from behind a shelter of rocks, took aim and picked out the officers, and fired. We first picked off all the leaders as they came up. What surprised us most and what we greatly admired was the bravery of your officers. They were too brave for this world, so we made angels of them. To us such bravery is marvellous, we cannot understand it; but it is not war.

As Macdonald comments, "This is very graphic, and expresses much truth. One can see in it a sarcastically coloured picture of what a British

---

[1] In this he followed in the footsteps of his uncle, Sir John, the Adjutant-General, who was noted for the close interest he took in his personnel at all levels – an unusual attribute in those days of extreme military formality.

colonel had got engrained in him by his own training, and what, in consequence of he and those above him having no imagination, the training of his battalion had been – to carry out a set of diagrammatic movements by stereotyped shouted words of command as if on a flat parade."

Macdonald wrote many articles, gave many addresses and engaged in much correspondence on the subject of reform. Among the chief publications was *Common Sense on Parade or Drill without Stays* published by Blackwood in 1886. In that year a new edition of the *Army Drill Book* was published; it had in his words "so grievously disappointed all who had hoped to see some advance made in the direction of simplicity, celerity, and convenience, and a larger part devoted to real battle training." He quotes from a multitude of military commanders and sources, French, German, Austrian, American, as well as British.[1] By the time *The Book* in its fully revised form appeared in 1902 no less than 146 out of 178 changes put forward in *Common Sense on Parade* had been adopted. "For the first time the practical took its place finally and completely in our infantry system, sending the fossil remains of the theatrical to the limbo from whence they can never come back."

Throughout he enjoyed the strong support of Field-Marshal Lord Wolseley and Sir Evelyn Wood, his friends over many years, both of whom saw that these reforms were introduced when they were in a position to do so, as Commander-in-Chief and Adjutant-General of the forces respectively. Both appreciated that Macdonald was able to bring more pressure to bear as a military outsider than as a regular. *Fifty Years of It* is dedicated to them both.

Needless to say, Macdonald encountered strong opposition from the old brigade over the years. "There goes the man that has ruined the drill of the British Army", said one, and the Duke of Cambridge, Commander-in-Chief, and a cousin of the Queen, was reported as muttering when he saw some manoeuvre done in a way new to him, although it was in the *Book* by his own 'Order': "That will be that *** Scotch lawyer again."

In the 1880s and 1890s Macdonald made annual excursions to the French and German autumn manoeuvres and visited some of the old

---

[1] There are well over 100 writers – military, political, literary – quoted in the text of *Fifty Years of It* or as chapter headings ranging from Shakespeare to Napoleon. He must have spent far more time on his military researches and writings than he did on many of his legal activities.

battlefields of the Franco-German War. At an earlier time he had gone
to the field of Waterloo, being particularly interested to see the place
where his uncle, Alexander Macdonald of the RHA (General Alick, as
he calls him), in command of an artillery battery "kept things so hot
that the story goes that Napoleon himself asked who it was that was
mowing down the attack." The only time Macdonald came close to an
actual battle-front during hostilities and heard the guns of war was in
1916 when he went to the grave of his son John at Bailleul, near Ypres.

It was his military achievements that brought the award of the KCB
in 1900 and the GCB in 1916. He was proud to receive the GCB, to em-
ulate his uncle, Sir John, the Adjutant-General.

One major invention resulted from his military manoeuvres ("war
games", he called them). He writes in *Fifty Years of It*:

> We had great trouble at first with the maps, owing to there
> being nothing but the contour lines to give guidance as to
> elevations, and so it was difficult to get a "coup-d'oeil" idea
> of the ground. I suggested to the Secretary (of the Tactical
> Society which organised the manoeuvres) that it would be a
> great improvement if the maps were coloured from a deep
> brown on the higher contours down to pale brown, and the
> lower ground from a pale green to a dark green. This was
> done and was much appreciated. All the publishers of tour-
> ing maps for cyclists and motorists have adopted the system.
> I do not suppose the idea was patentable, and if it had been
> that it would have brought me any gain; but it certainly must
> be a great benefit to all who use maps for practical locomo-
> tion, and might also be used with advantage in schools.

Chapter 14

The Most Versatile Scotsman of his Times

Even leaving aside his legal, political and military activities, the range and depth of Macdonald's interests are quite remarkable. He saw early on the many possible uses of electricity, and in his customary thorough way studied and promoted practical means for its development for the benefit of all. "This subject interested me deeply and I lectured on it as a young man to a great many audiences in town and country." He described the use of electricity for mechanical purposes as "most useful step of progress of our time." In 1882 he wrote an article in *Blackwood's Magazine* on *Electric Progress*, setting out what had been achieved already and, greatly inspired (if not dazzled) by the manifold appliances and effects he had seen at the recent Exposition in Paris, indicating likely future developments. On the historical side he has a characteristic criticism of the doubters:

> It is in the history of electricity itself that the most extraordinary instances are to be found of the narrow-mindedness and want of foresight, even of learned men, in regard to the practicability and usefulness of discoveries and inventions … In 1879 scientific men declared it would be found impossible to adapt electric lighting to dwelling-houses or small rooms. In the same year one of the most able and experienced electricians of the day stated, before a Select Committee, that he did not think the telephone would be very much used in this country.

In an 1895 Address to the Royal Scottish Society of Arts (of which he was a past President) on *Electricity in the Dwelling* he demonstrated with great technical detail and the help of various appliances and illustrations just how electricity could be used for different purposes domestically. His house in Abercromby Place was among the first (if not the first) in Edinburgh to have full electric lighting.

Among his many inventions was an Electric Holophote Course Indicator, designed to prevent collisions at sea by means of a powerful arc light on the helm of a ship with a strong reflector behind it, which could be turned to indicate by the movement of the beam of light the direction in which the ship was steering. Hitherto with only the lights on port and starboard this was not possible. This invention won an award at the Crystal Palace Electrical Exhibition in 1882, one of a number of awards for inventions he won, nationally and internationally (from the King of the Belgians and the US government). His other inventions included a Military Field Telegraph system and a Barothermotelemeter.

He wrote to Gladstone in 1869 urging the introduction of a halfpenny stamped post-card, and pursued this with the Post Office. It was introduced the following year.

He was a leading pioneer of motoring and well ahead of his time in foreseeing the development of the motor car and the need for a proper roads system. He wrote and spoke widely on these and related topics. He was among the very first owners of a motor car in Scotland, a founder member and Steward of the Automobile Club of Great Britain and Ireland (later the Royal Automobile Club), and first President of the Scottish (later Royal Scottish) Automobile Club, founded in 1899. He took part in "the first great demonstration of the practicability of mechanical road locomotion", the 1000 miles tour from London to Edinburgh and back in 1900. When motor registration marks were first introduced in 1903 he became the owner of the number S1, the first number for Edinburgh.[1] He was for many years an active member of HM Road Board which was responsible for all matters relating to roads and their use, from the best surfacing to road signs and the rules of the road. Macdonald would be in his element in such deliberations.

There are many accounts by him and others of his early motoring experiences. An especially interesting one, entitled *The Good Girl*, appeared in the *Motor-Car Journal* in 1901 in which he describes the

[1] (See Illustrations)

journey, at a maximum speed of about 20mph, in his new Delahaye (fitted out with the latest improvements including several of his own invention) from Paris, where he had picked it up, to Edinburgh. His numerous articles in the *Car Magazine* and other journals, and lectures included such titles as: *A Hundred Miles on a Benz*; *Road Driving – Animal and Motor Contrasted*; *Motor-Cars for Coast Defence*; *Road Signs and Warnings – A Plea for Uniformity*; and *Retrospect and Prospect: 1900-1910 and After*.

In 1904 a motor company built the *Kingsburgh*; designed as a motor-bus carrying twelve passengers, it plied its trade between Waverley and Haymarket stations for a brief time.

TB Simpson in his privately printed *Dry Fun: Parliament House Characters* describes Macdonald's car as "a sort of petrol-driven wagonette with solid rubber tyres", and he narrates the story about the Lord Justice-Clerk on one of his early drives being thrown out of his car, landing on his head on the road. "It's a mercy", said an advocate, "that he didn't land on his bottom. He might have dashed his brains out." Simpson quotes a nickname apparently used for Sir John: "The Motoring Mormon".

Macdonald wrote a fictional story, *Vanessa: A Motor Idyll,* which appeared as a serial in *Chambers's Journal* in 1909. A romantic tale about Vanessa, a young heiress and orphan of "ineffable charm", and her motoring adventures on the road, it is narrated in the first person by Mary, a younger (about sixteen years old) doting admirer of Vanessa. Macdonald carries this off very credibly as if comfortable within the young girl's mind. His style is much freer than in his non-fictional writings. At the end of one episode he writes about how youth can help to inspire love: "The breezy unconventionality of youthfulness seems sometimes by its presence to change the atmosphere from the chokiness of social etiquette to a more free-breath tone".

One cannot but wonder how much of his late wife is projected in the idealised person of Vanessa. There are physical similarities – Vanessa, like Adelaide, being tall for her sex, and her hair generally worn "coiled in a crown round her head", Vanessa's newly discovered godfather (Major Goodman) tells Mary how seeing his godchild had reminded him of her mother with whom he had been in love many years before: "To-day I saw her every feature, her every charm, as vividly as if thirty years were but yesterday. And that voice, that warbling tone like the murmur of a sweet brook, it carried me back to the old days, and my poor old heart beat wildly". It was over thirty years since Adelaide's death, and one can sense Sir John bringing her to fictional life in many of the characteristics of Vanessa, and placing her in the later times of motor-cars.

He saw the advantages of the use of motor vehicles in war and gave a lecture on this which spurred the War Office to action. He was the first to use motor transport for purely military purposes at one of his brigade camps, an example soon followed by German, French and British Generals. He took an active interest in the Army Motor Reserve (of which he was Honorary Colonel) and in motor ambulances during the First War. Soon after war broke out his son Jack volunteered for service in France, where he went with a specially designed autocar ambulance; later he was put in charge of a fleet of ambulances under the Red Cross.

✳

Throughout his life Macdonald held a great interest in education. He gave the inaugural address of the Watt Institution Literary Association for 1875 on *The Higher Aims of Education*. Quoting William Cowper he stresses the emptiness of knowledge without wisdom:

> *Knowledge and wisdom, far from being one,*
> *Have ofttimes no connection. Knowledge dwells*
> *In heads replete with thoughts of other men,*
> *Wisdom in minds attentive to their own.*

At school, Macdonald said, " the standards are fixed by so much reading and writing" up to a low minimum level only, not conducive to success as regards the higher aims. And if a child wishes to go on to further studies, a "good crammer" is sought "to fatten him up in haste, that by his large number of points he may take a prize in the Intellectual Cattle Show", the result producing a mass of "overloaded mental plethora".

The "higher aims", in Macdonald's words, are to:

> Train the young to habits of self-subjugation, self-examination

and self-sacrifice, on the one hand, and true self-reliance and self-culture, on the other, that a man may be brought to the condition so well described by Wordsworth, in which he knows that:

True knowledge leads to love:
True dignity abides with him alone
Who in the silent hour of inward thought
Can still suspect and still revere himself
In lowliness of heart.

He argued that religious instruction at school must play a part. He ends his address by enjoining his listeners not to let their care for their children's education stop at:

mere intellectual improvements and external polish. Give them some of your society daily, join in their sport, take an interest in their amusements, however childish ... And above all things keep in view that as Goethe says (Macdonald's translation):

What only shines has but a moment's stay;
The real lasts out the new earth's endless day.

He was concerned at the decline of Gaelic speaking and supported the need for its teaching, not in the same way as other languages, but to give sufficient understanding of the language. He sat on the Privy Council on Education from 1885-89, and on the Edinburgh University Court from 1889; he was a Director (latterly Chairman) of The Edinburgh Academy Directors from 1881 until his death in 1919.

Another great enthusiasm of Macdonald's was amateur dramatics. He took part in the 1870s in performances at the house of Professor and Mrs Fleeming Jenkin, where Robert Louis Stevenson (a protégé of the Professor) also often performed. Macdonald describes in *Life Jottings* how once, not at the Jenkins' but at the Misses Mairs' (great-granddaughters of Sarah Siddons), he played the part of Shylock to Stevenson's Antonio in the trial scene from *The Merchant of Venice*. Stevenson was a young advocate at that time when Macdonald knew him well, and he writes that Stevenson:

> paid me the compliment of saying afterwards that the expression of "lodged hate", as interpreted in my face, was convincing. He and I walked home together that night, and severely criticised some performances of others, as possibly others did ours. I little thought then that I was side by side with one who was to carry forward the literary fame of Edinburgh into yet another generation. I never saw him again after that night.

In a letter to his father in 1874, Stevenson, referring to Macdonald's candidature for Parliament in opposition to the Lord Provost, Duncan McLaren, wrote: "Macdonald's sentiments are quite good. I would support him against McLaren at once". Macdonald was described in his day as "the drama-loving" Lord Advocate; he is said to have written some plays anonymously, and he was known as a very good mimic. There is an amusing portrait of him dressed as Meg Dods from Scott's *St Ronan's Well*, presumably for some amateur theatricals. His son Jack went on the professional stage at one time in his varied career and acted with Lewis Waller's company.

Macdonald knew well various artists – among them Charles Doyle, Sir George Reid and Fiddes Watt (who did four portraits of him at different times). A very sensitive portrait of him in his seventies was painted by Sir Hubert von Herkomer for the Royal Automobile Club in London.[1] Herkomer was a remarkably interesting man with a great diversity of artistic achievements. His early, Social Realist, work was admired by Van Gogh who refers to him in his letters. He came to England from Bavaria to study art and settled in London. He worked as a painter and as "an engraver, wood-carver, ironsmith, architect, journalist, playwright, composer, singer and actor" (*Cambridge Biographical Encyclopedia*), also setting up a film studio where he was a pioneer of silent film. In 1889 he was appointed Slade Professor of Fine Art at Oxford. His portrait paintings included Wagner, Ruskin, Lord

---

[1] (See Illustrations)

Kelvin, Queen Victoria and Kaiser Willhelm III. He was interested in motoring and joined the Royal Automobile Club in 1904. He initiated the Herkomer Trophy as a prize for a touring rally in Germany in conjunction with the Bavarian Automobile Club, making it a condition that the winner was painted by him. The portrait of Sir John must have been done quite separately from this. It was presented to the Royal Automobile Club by the artist. He and Sir John, with such an immense range of activities between them, must have had some engrossing exchanges during their sittings.

At his house in Abercromby Place Macdonald had a large collection of pictures, many inherited from his father, including no less than fifty-five paintings by the Rev John Thomson of Duddingston. In his will he directed that all his pictures, other than portraits or those specifically bequeathed, should be sold. His step-mother, Agnes Hume, had inherited two portraits of her great-uncle, David Hume, by Allan Ramsay, one of which she donated to the National Gallery of Scotland and which has hung in the Scottish National Portrait Gallery since its founding; the other, having been kept in the family, recently joined it there.

In addition to his rifle-shooting activities, already described, John Macdonald had many other sporting interests; he lists among his recreations golf, cricket, lawn tennis, curling, rugby football and athletics. He had little scope for sports in his school days; neither school he attended had any playing fields. His most pleasant recollection of the Circus Place school, which he left aged 9, was the training he got in gymnastics and fencing. At the Edinburgh Academy there were no organised games. Most play was in "The Yards" in front of the main school building – "an expanse of loose gravel, the marks of falls on which I still bear upon my knees". The boys played improvised games, including one called "hailes" unique to the Academy. A cross between hockey and shinty, played with clackens – "wooden long-handled bats with round-headed ends like flattened spoons", as described by Magnus Magnusson in his history of the Academy, "The Clacken and the Slate".

The game consists largely of a series of melees between two teams at close quarters, a "hail" being scored when one side drives the ball against the wall defended by the opposing team.

Facilities improved after his schooldays. By the time he returned from his studies in Switzerland aged 19, his old school had acquired playing fields at Raeburn Place, where "the Academy boys disport themselves in costumes in two great fields, each with its pavilion, with lavatory and even baths." Organised matches were played every week, and full-scale annual sports days were held. Teams often travelled long distances to play against other schools – something unheard of in his boyhood. "I think I can hear my father, if such a proposal had been made for his sanction, and the producing of the necessary rail fare, say in decisive tones: 'The match of that for absurdity I never heard'. There was not much of the *nos mutatur* in him". John felt that the attitude to change of his father and many like him was "What was good enough for me, must be good enough for you". How very different from his own fresh independent outlook and practical sense which enabled him to see the benefits of innovations and improvements in so many areas of life.

On his return to Edinburgh he threw himself into playing rugby football and cricket. In 1858, along with his friend, William Blackwood and thirteen others he founded the Edinburgh Academical Football Club, the first Rugby Football Club in Scotland. He describes playing:

> Twenty-a-side, and a scrum was a scrum indeed – fifteen pushing against fifteen in a tight maul, which often was im-movable for several minutes. The steam rose from the pack like the smoke from a charcoal-burner's pile. It was much more straining and fatiguing than the more open game of to-day. During the years of my football work I was never able to cross one leg over another on a Sunday if I had been playing a match on the previous Saturday, and as for shins the breaking up of a maul when it came meant vigorous kicking ahead, on the chance that ball and toe might meet.

One of his fellow players told how, when lying on the ball and hacking were allowed, Macdonald used to lie on the ball and ignore the hack-ing if his side needed a breather. They had "not much luxury"; their only pavilion was "a small loft over an outhouse in the garden of a villa in the corner of the field, approached by a wooden ladder." In his speech at the Club's Jubilee Dinner in 1908, at which he proposed the health of "The Four Football Unions", he gave an even more graphic description of a scrum in the early days: "Very few of you have seen a real scrum. Have you ever seen a haycock that was put up when the hay was wet, and the smoke or steam was rising from it fourteen or fifteen feet into the air? That was just what a scrum was in those days – absolutely still and steaming". They played in any old clothes and had no basins or lockers. The only thing they could do after a match "was to go up into that loft and smoke until it was sufficiently dark and we could go through the streets without being mobbed".

The first Rugby International against England took place at Raeburn Place in 1871. Macdonald sat at the entrance gate behind a deal table collecting the gate money of a shilling per head in an earthenware bowl. The crowd was estimated variously between 2,000 and 4,000.

Following a dispute over the interpretation of a ruling in the Scotland v England game in 1884, the fixture did not take place the next year, nor did England play any of the other three countries in 1888 and 1889. The English Rugby Union wished to retain their position as the makers of the rules for the game, while the Scottish, Irish and Welsh Unions sat on an International Board, which was set up, but not recognised by the English. It was not until the end of 1889 that the English RU agreed to submit the matter to arbitration by two arbiters – Lord Kingsburgh, the Lord Justice-Clerk, and Major Francis Marindin, President of the Football Association. The result was the setting up of the International Rugby Football Board as regulator and administrator of the code of laws for all Internationals. The English came out of it well by having six members on the board, as opposed to the other three Unions with two each. For their services each arbiter was presented with a handsome silver rose bowl decorated with emblems of the four home countries.[1]

He was an enthusiastic golfer: a member of the Royal & Ancient (St Andrews), Luffness New, of which he was a founder member, and Wimbledon. One of his playing partners was Peter Guthrie Tait, who had been four years ahead of him at the Academy, but with whom

[1] Macdonald bequeathed his to the Edinburgh Academy as a challenge cup "to be awarded annually to the successful competitor or team competitors' captain, in any sporting, or military or musketry competition" the selection of the competition in each year to be decided by the Trustees of his will.

he became friendly many years later when Tait had become Professor of Natural Philosophy at Edinburgh University. "He and I became
good friends, and in the late Seventies I have played golf with him at
St. Andrews at six in the morning, a time when no other player would
turn out, and when no caddy thought it worth his while to get up so
early to earn the fee of a round, so we had to carry our own clubs." Tait
experimented with different clubs of his invention, and studied the
flight of golf balls and other dynamics of the game. Macdonald records
how proud Tait was of his son, Freddy, who was twice British Amateur
golf champion in the late 1890s, but was killed in 1900 in the Boer War,
and tells how his son's sad death shortened the life of his father, who
died the following year.

Macdonald was Captain of the R&A in 1887-8, and took a leading
part in the revision of the rules of Golf at that time. There is a charm-
ing picture of him in 1887 at the 9th hole at St Andrews being served
refreshment (probably ginger beer) from a wicker cart by a bearded
old caddy, drawn by "my friend Mr Hodge".[1] Macdonald was quite
an all-rounder: with his large "juggler's hands" he excelled as a fielder
in cricket, and he was also President of the Scottish Amateur Athletics
Association.

A key component in John Macdonald's life was his membership of the
Catholic Apostolic Church. Much of the doctrine of the Church sprang
from two very remarkable men – Edward Irving and Henry Drummond. As Minister of the Scots Church in London in the 1820s, Irving, a man of great charisma, held considerable influence and attracted
a huge following. As a result of the French Revolution and the tur-
bulent times that followed there was a conviction, strongly held by
Irving, that the Second Coming of the Lord was at hand. Instances of
"speaking with tongues" and of prophecy, which were occurring at
the time in Irving's congregation and elsewhere, were taken as man-
ifestations of this, and of the need for the Church to be prepared.
These views were shared by Henry Drummond, a wealthy London
banker, land owner and MP, who from 1826 held annual religious

---

[1] (See Illustrations)

conferences at his home, Albury Park in Surrey. This led to the formation of the Catholic Apostolic Church and the appointment of twelve Apostles (including Drummond himself), each with his own "tribe", to prepare for the imminent Second Coming. The Church was open to all baptised Christians and many Catholics, Methodists, Episcopalians and Presbyterians joined. As Lord Sands notes:

> In this Church there is not the same division between lay and clerical life as in most of the Churches. A member may stand high in their hierarchy and take a prominent part in the conduct of the services of the Church whilst still continuing to pursue the avocations of ordinary civil life. Such was Macdonald's position. One of the merits of this communion is that its members are always content to take the second best if they cannot get the best. If they cannot get their own service they are content to worship with other Christians. So wherever Macdonald went he had a Church to attend. His Catholicity was not of the type which unchurches every fellow-Christian whose pattern is not exactly as one's own.

Like many reformers with a strong popular following (his being known as Irvingites), Irving fell foul of the powers that be in the Established Presbyterian Church, and in March 1833 he was stripped of his ministry. Many from his large congregation followed him to new Church premises in London, and in April he was ordained an "Angel" of the Catholic Apostolic Church by the first Apostle, John Cardale. Irving died the following year.

Churches were set up in Europe (including seven in London), North America and Australia, each congregation with an Angel (chief Pastor) at the head, and priests and deacons.

John's father, Mathew Norman Macdonald, was a founder member of the Church in Edinburgh and from 1856 an Angel – lay members, who undertook much pastoral work, being eligible for such ordainment. He would probably know Irving personally from meeting him at the home of his friend and relative, James Bridges, where Irving stayed when in Edinburgh. John followed in his father's footsteps. He became Archdeacon for Scotland; as such he had many administrative functions, assisted by Deacons. This included overseeing the Church buildings and finances, and supervisor of the theological content of the Phoebe Traquair murals in the Church at Mansfield Place, Edinburgh. In her guide to the building, now known as the Mansfield Traquair Centre, Elizabeth Cumming writes: "He (John Macdonald) guided the work closely, specifying the subject matter and approving the artist's proposals. He shared the belief of both the artist herself and the Social Union that the 'arts express ideas and feelings as powerful as words can do'". He is known to have travelled to Australia (part of his "tribe" as Archdeacon) in the 1890s, where Irving's grand-daughter recalled him visiting her family in Melbourne when she was a young girl. He also visited Toronto in 1904 for the Church convention there.

In 1895 John was appointed an Archangel, receiving his blessing at Albury from the last surviving Apostle, FV Woodhouse. As Archangel he gave theological advice and assistance; as the one representative in Scotland of the Universal Church this was an important role, especially after the death of Woodhouse in 1901, which led to difficulties in holding together the various Churches in Britain and abroad. The Second Coming was expected imminently and no provision for succession and continuity had been made. Ordinations continued by Church leaders, but they lacked the divine force of the apostolate blessing. With the numbers of those who could officiate dwindling the Church went into decline over the next decades, and by the early 1960s almost all Churches were closed. In Edinburgh services ceased in 1953, and the building was sold. Fortunately the Traquair murals, which had suffered severely from dampness and neglect have been conserved and painstakingly restored in all their colourful glory, and they remain highly symbolic works of art in the Church where followers of this rare religion worshipped, with such high but ultimately unfulfilled expectations.

John Macdonald's faith and practice permeated his life and work. The tenets of the Church encouraged acceptance of what you have – gentleness, not thrusting ambition or elbowing."Tread the earth lightly" was a precept he would follow. In his judicial work a tension must have existed for him between the mildness of God's law, for example in the exercise of mercy, as against the severity of earthly law. Most especially this is manifest in his feelings and conduct when he had to pronounce the ultimate sentence of the death penalty.

He makes no mention of his religion in his writings.

Chapter 15

Last Years

After his retiral as Lord Justice-Clerk in 1915 Macdonald remained very active in many fields. His *Life Jottings of an Old Edinburgh Citizen* was published in October of that year and he continued in various public positions, especially on HM Road Board.

During the Great War in an article for *Chambers's Journal: Dover Tunnel and the Scottish Ship Canal* he strongly supported the proposal for a Channel Tunnel, and added the suggestion of having a Forth and Clyde Canal. He wrote of the benefits for commerce as well as leisure travel – moving goods and passengers – in having a rail journey with electric traction through a tunnel which would be at least one and a half hours quicker and considerably easier. And, as he says, it would have helped greatly with the movement of troops and supplies to the war front. He answers the criticism that previously prevailed over the vulnerability during wartime of its use by enemy forces, by pointing out that the situation had fundamentally changed since Wellington's day, when the idea was first mooted and the French were then the enemy, and how any military danger of troops emerging from the narrow defile at the end of the tunnel and any invasion by sea or land could be readily defended.

A Forth and Clyde Canal, he writes, would allow vessels, naval (and he includes the largest ships) or otherwise, to move from one coast of Scotland across to the other with clear advantages, military and commercial, avoiding the long journey round Land's End or Shetland.

Both proposals, he states at the end of the article, if carried out, would help towards having better preparedness than for the present war, when " the nation was found poorly prepared … and as a natural consequence has suffered inordinately both in blood and treasure."

Like so very many he personally suffered close family loss; his son Jack was killed at the front in France in March 1916. He had inherited his father's taste for mechanics and motoring, and soon after war broke out he volunteered for service in France, where he drove a specially designed car ambulance, rescuing and removing the wounded. Some of the most graphic narratives in the London papers came from him. He was later in charge of a fleet of ambulances under the British Red Cross Society, and then played a large part at the Front in the work of the Graves Royal Commission (which became the War Graves Commission) as a Captain. This work involved not only the care of graves and cemeteries, but the marking and recording of every grave accessible within the lines. It was while engaged in this work that he was killed by a shell-burst on the Ypres-Menin road. He was 49. For his work in the front line he was mentioned in Despatches. A young cousin, only 19, was killed in France a few months later; he was Lieutenant Norman Martin of the Cameron Highlanders, who had won the DSO a year earlier. At the age of 18 he was the youngest to have won that honour.

In June 1916, aged 79, Macdonald went on a pilgrimage to his son's grave, a journey described in his account *To Somewhere in France and Back* published in two parts in *Chambers's Journal*. Keeping his emotions firmly unexpressed he does not even refer to his son, merely telling of visiting "the place of rest of one who gave his life in fulfilling his duty".

He was accompanied by the Director of the Graves Registration Unit, a Colonel, who was going over to his headquarters in France. He was advised to wear uniform to help getting through check-points, and to lessen the possibility of being suspected as a spy, so he donned his full suit of khaki, as worn by his old Volunteers corps. He describes the rough Channel crossing and the journey by car to the HQ, passing innumerable troops and transport vehicles. Parts looked like "the temporary Anglicising" of the country, with football and cricket games, even a van bearing on its sides "LENA ASHWELL'S FIRING-LINE CONCERT PARTY", "a symbol", he says, "of that unselfish ministering by the theatrical profession to the cheering-up of the soldier returning for a rest from the fatigues and horrors of the trenches, which doubtless wards off many a nervous breakdown."

He and his companion arrived at where Sir Douglas Haig had his

HQ, well behind the firing-line. They then went forward towards the front, reaching the Colonel's HQ. There he was hospitably received by colleagues of his son, including a Major who was "a close comrade of him who was gone". He escorted Macdonald to Bailleul, nearer the front, and to his son's grave in the British war cemetery there. He was touched to find that a French family, who had become close friends of his son, "brightened the spot with fresh flowers", and he laid there some flowers from Jack's home and a sprig of white heather.

Returning from Bailleul he saw and heard signs of the war:

> By going up to the top of a rising ground it was possible to see Ypres and Popperinghe … The great church tower of Ypres was seen still standing in the midst of a once attractive town laid in ruins. This view had a special melancholy interest, as it was in front of Ypres that he whose resting-place had just been visited was locating a grave near a trench, and met a bursting shell which brought him to his end.

The knowledge that his son fell while engaged on this work must have added to the poignancy of the visit to the grave.

He writes of great contrasts:

> In looking towards Ypres … All seemed to speak of a peaceful countryside. But as one gazed, the serenity of the scene was marred by the sight of 'sausage' balloons at rest in the air for observation, and by bursts of smoke rising in columns near the town as shells exploded, followed to the ear by the boom of the great guns which caused the marring of the sweetness of the landscape.

It was the only time in his life that he heard the guns of war fired in earnest.

Macdonald did his bit for the war effort. He acted as Drill Sergeant to the local Territorials in Perth, near Auchterarder, where he stayed much of the time at his son and daughter-in-law's house; as he says in *Life Jottings*, "grinding them as I did when I trained my company fifty-five years ago".

He lived to see the end of the war, but survived only until May 1919, when he died at his home, 15 Abercromby Place, from heart failure after a brief illness. He was 82. By an odd twist of fate he was to have received the Freedom of the City of Edinburgh on the day of his death. The ceremony had been postponed from an earlier date due to the illness of another recipient. In his last years he was recognised as the Grand Old Man of Edinburgh, and the funeral was a big public occasion. After a service in the Catholic Apostolic Church, the procession, with the coffin on a gun carriage and headed by two companies of Edinburgh Academy cadets, moved along crowd-lined streets, the traffic having been stopped all the way to St Cuthbert's Churchyard at the west end of Princes Street, where he was laid to rest. The Lord Provost walked at the side of the gun carriage as one of the pall-bearers. At the graveside pipers played the lament *The Land o' the Leal*.

Macdonald's Printed Works

Autobiographical:

Life Jottings of an old Edinburgh Citizen	TN Foulis 1915	*passim*

Fiction:

Our Trip to Blunderland	Blackwood 1877	75-7
Vanessa: A Motor Idyll	Chambers' Journal 1909	190-92

Motoring and Roads:

The Good Girl	Motor-Car Journal 1901	190-91
The Road and the Power Vehicle	Chambers' Journal	
Present and Future of Motor Traction	Address to the RSSA 1901	
Suggestions for Autocar Accessories	do.	
Auto-cars	Address to the Royal Institution of GB 1902	
A Hundred Miles on a Benz	The Car Magazine 1902	191
Road Driving:		
Animal and Motor Contrasted	do.	191
The Rule of the Road	do. 1903	
Motor-Cars for Coast Defence	do. 1906	191
Power Traction on Roads	do. 1907	
Road Signs and Warnings:		
A Plan for Uniformity	do. 1908	191
The Road – The Question of the Day	do. 1908	
Motor-Cars and Land Defence	do. 1909	
Retrospect and Prospect: 1900-1910	do. 1910	191
Savants and the Road	Address to the Royal Institution 1912	

Main Archival Sources

National Archives of Scotland (formerly Scottish Record Office).
Scottish office papers: Lord Advocate papers, Lothian Muniments

National Library of Scotland
Blackwood papers

Signet Library, Edinburgh
Scots Law Times and other Scottish legal journals and records;
William Roughhead Collection

Mitchell Library, Glasgow
City of Glasgow Bank papers

Clan Donald Library, Armadale, Isle of Skye
Clan Donald genealogies and other papers

Edinburgh University Library
Hansard Parliamentary Reports; Blackwood Magazines

Peebles Library
Papers re: Hay family

Wexford County Library
Papers re Doran and Hughes families

Edinburgh City Archives

Black Watch Museum, Perth

Beaulieu Motor Museum
Various motoring articles

Gordon Square Church, London
Catholic Apostle Church archive

Acknowledgements

This book has been a long time in the making, as many who have shown an interest in it will be well aware. I expect some will have given up hope of ever seeing it in print. It would be impossible to recall all those who have provided support and information and encouraged (in some cases cajoled) me in my endeavours over the years. To all I would record my thanks. Sadly, many have died, some of whom gave me personal reminiscences of Sir John, including the Very Rev Ronald Selby Wright, Ranald Hume Macdonald (a grandson), Colin Simpson and the Rev Dr FR Stevenson; also, most interestingly, Edward Irving's grand-daughter Helen Campbell who I met when she was 103 years old, her mind fully alert. She recalled Sir John visiting her family in Melbourne, Australia, when she was a young girl and he was there in his capacity as an Archdeacon of the Catholic Apostolic Church, the members in Australia being part of his "tribe"

I am especially indebted to my editor, Duncan Lockerbie, for all his enthusiastic assistance in the production and publication of the work.

Above all, my wife Jill has been my mainstay through all the vicissitudes along the way.

Selected Index